THE
ALLOTMENT
GARDENER'S
HANDBOOK

THE ALLOTMENT GARDENER'S HANDBOOK

Alan Titchmarsh

With drawings by Patricia Capon

SEVERN
HOUSE

In memory of my grandfathers – gardeners both

British Library Cataloguing in Publication Data

Titchmarsh, Alan, 1949–
   The allotment gardener's handbook.
   1. Gardening   2. Working-men's gardens
   1. Title
   635   SB453

   ISBN 0-7278-2026-5

Published by Severn House
Publishers Limited
4 Brook Street
London W1Y 1AA

Editorial   Ian Jackson and
             Diana Levinson
Design   Camron Design Limited
          and Keith Lovegrove

Back cover photograph of Alan
Titchmarsh © Bob Belton/
Woman's Own

Typeset by TJB Photosetting,
South Witham, Lincs.

Printed and bound by Hazell
Watson and Viney Ltd., Aylesbury,
Buckinghamshire

CONTENTS

ACKNOWLEDGEMENTS

My thanks are due to a handful of individuals who have been of great help during the preparation of this book. To Mr Weston and Mr McGarry of the Royal Borough of Windsor & Maidenhead Amenities Department I am grateful for information on allotment regulations. Donald McLean, Britain's most expert potato grower, supplied advice on growing show potatoes, and other unsuspecting vegetable growers have given sundry tips and wrinkles when cornered at flower shows over the past five years! Most of the methods described have been put into practice on my own allotment and home vegetable plots, and I must thank my wife for bravely tasting a few unusual vegetables and for exercising her patience while this book was written. Diana Levinson and Ian Jackson also deserve a special 'thank you' for their boundless enthusiasm and encouragement.

INTRODUCTION

I was two when I encountered my first allotment; it was my grandfather's and it ran down a slope on the banks of the River Wharfe in Yorkshire. It was a magical plot packed with a child's delights – blackberries scrambled over brass bedsteads, peas climbed up barricades of twigs and silvery chocolate tins dangled on strings to frighten away the sparrows. Most exciting of all were a seemingly bottomless tank of sootwater nettles and scrap metal.

Allotment gardening is a more risky business than gardening at home. Vandalism and theft may cause problems (they always have) but seldom will the grower lose too much of his produce provided he keeps his tempting asparagus and raspberries some distance away from the public path!

With so many tools, chemicals and other aids, the gardener's lot

sunk into the ground and a crippled and spooky shed. The first was used for watering the rhubarb and the second contained a mixture of battered tools, bonemeal and spilled seeds.

Nowadays many allotments are not much different. The bedsteads and chocolate tins have gone but the battered tools and bonemeal remain. So too does the great sense of achievement at cultivating food on a piece of ground that would otherwise harbour docks,

can be easier than it was 30 years ago when my grandfather tilled the soil. It can also be more confusing. This book aims to help the allotment gardener to produce the best crops from his land all the year round without being frightened by complicated techniques and lethal-sounding chemical applications, and without having to spend every waking hour tending to his crops and turning his soil.

Alan Titchmarsh
Beech, 1982

1 THE ALLOTMENT

The dictionary neatly defines an allotment as: 'a small plot of land let out by a public authority to individuals for gardening, especially vegetable growing'. Thanks to the official-sounding *Small Holdings and Allotments Act* 1908 (Section 23) and the *Allotments Act* 1950 (Section 9), there is a statutory obligation for local authorities to provide allotments for the use of ratepayers, and many local councils now accommodate a growing band of keen gardeners.

In the mid-1970s the self-sufficiency craze urged many folk to demand allotments with the result that waiting lists lengthened dramatically. Now that the initial burst of enthusiasm has died down, there is still a queue for plots in most areas but numbers are usually in two figures rather than three.

The first thing to do if you want an allotment is to contact the Amenities Department of your local Council by telephone to enquire about the availability and location of their plots. Before you decide to spice your spare time with a hefty patch of unturned earth, make sure that you can afford to make two or three visits to the plot each week. If it is too far away you will soon find plenty of excuses not to visit it regularly, which means that when you do get there you will have to strive constantly to beat the weeds and the pests. This type of allotment gardening is no fun!

Some Councils will have the plot roughly cultivated before it is handed over to a new tenant; others will not bother but are sometimes willing to arrange a reduced rental in the first year of tenancy.

If you decide that an allotment is for you, have your name put on the waiting list if necessary and then write to confirm your request. Don't be put off if you are told that 50 names are already on the list. At least half that number will back out when they are offered an allotment and others may have left the district and forgotten to remove their names. It need not be too long before your name comes up.

Allotments are rented on a yearly basis and are usually measured in rods, poles or perches which gives them rather a rustic flavour. Rods, poles and perches are three words for the same measurement, each denoting about 5m or 16½ft. Have a look at the size of plot you are likely to be offered before you agree to take it on – it will be larger than you think!

Rents vary tremendously from place to place but most will make a reduction for old age pensioners – often in the region of 50%. (One sample price charged by a London borough is £1-50 per rod with a rate of £0-36 for pensioners.)

RULES AND REGULATIONS

The Council will require you to sign a Tenancy Agreement which will stipulate the rules and regulations to be observed by an allotment holder and which will indicate works and provisions that will be made by the local authority.

The following points are made in the Tenancy Agreement supplied by the Royal Borough of Windsor and Maidenhead and are typical of the conditions with which most allotment holders will have to comply. They are given here purely as an example and although they are correct at the time of writing they may, of course, be altered and amended at any time. The basic principles are unlikely to change:

1 Rent must be paid on time.
2 The plot must be cultivated and kept free of weeds.
3 Paths must be kept clean and tidy.
4 No nuisance must be caused to other allotment holders.
5 No subletting of the plot must take place without the prior permission of the Council.
6 No established trees surrounding the plot must be pruned without Council permission, and no soil or turf etc., taken away.
7 No buildings must be erected without prior permission and if permission is given the building should not measure more than 2.5m (8ft) by 1.25m (4ft).
8 All access gates must be kept closed when not in use.
9 Water must not be wasted.
10 The allotment must not be used for trade or business.
11 No refuse (apart from compost or manure in reasonable quantity) must be deposited on or around the plot.
12 No barbed wire must be used in fencing the plot.
13 Trees may only be planted with the permission of the Council.
14 Dogs must be kept on a lead.
15 No livestock must be kept on the plot except bees.
16 No notice or advertisement should be erected.
17 The Council has the right to refuse admission to any person attending the plot unless that person is accompanied by the tenant or a member of the tenant's family.
18 Disputes between tenants will be referred to the Council whose decision is final.
19 The Council must be informed if the tenant changes his address.
20 If allotment buildings are not kept in good repair in spite of a written request by the Council, then the Council has the right to remove and dispose of them.

Provision is also made for the allotments to be visited at any time by a member of the Council or the Council's agent.

The Council itself agrees to fulfil the following obligations:

1 To provide and maintain a piped water supply to the allotments.
2 To maintain existing roads to the site.
3 To maintain boundary hedges, fences and gates to the site.
4 To maintain all watercourses and ditches under the Council's control running through or near the allotment site.
5 To maintain existing land drains.

TERMINATION OF TENANCY

Should the tenant wish to terminate the agreement he must give the Council 14 days' notice in writing.

Should the Council wish to terminate the agreement they must give the tenant 12 months' notice in writing. Such notice will be arranged to expire on or before 6 April or on or after 29 September in any year.

However, should the land be required for building, mining, roadworks, mains laying, sewer construction or industrial purposes, three months' notice may be given once planning permission has been obtained.

The tenant will be given one month's notice to quit if he fails to pay the rent for more than 40 days after the agreed date; if he fails to comply with the rules; if he commits any act of bankruptcy; if he is convicted of pilfering from the allotment site. The tenancy is also relinquished if the tenant dies.

2
EQUIPPING THE PLOT

Before you lift a spade to cut the first sod on your newly acquired allotment, ensure that the plot is equipped with the basic facilities which will make cultivation and access reasonably easy.

ACCESS

There should already be a network of paths between the allotments, but make sure that the sections around your own plot are sound and level so that pushing a wheelbarrow is not a bone-rattling chore. Level out bumps and hollows and repair broken-down edges by cutting out a square of turf and reversing it so that the broken edge is replaced with a clean one. Cut down overgrown grass on paths and make a neat, straight edge by cutting vertically with a spade against a taut garden line.

WATERING

It may well be autumn or winter when you come to take over your plot, but do not forget that in dry summers many crops will require copious amounts of water if they are to continue growing and maturing. A good allotment site will be equipped with a mains water supply and plenty of taps to make the transport of water to any plot relatively easy. In such circumstances a hosepipe (either individually or communally owned) is all that is needed to direct the water where it is required.

Some allotment sites are provided with just one tap. This is fine for the person whose plot is positioned alongside it, but hard luck on the gardener at the opposite end of the allotments. If he can afford a hosepipe long enough to reach his plot, all he will get out of it is a measly trickle when

Broken path edges can easily be repaired if a slab of turf is cut out and then reversed so that the damaged edge lies on the inside. It will not be long before the scar is soon masked when the grass grows.

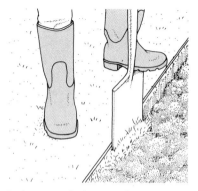

Rather ragged edges can be straightened by slicing them cleanly with a spade held against a taut garden line.

the tap is turned on. If he uses a watering can he will quickly tire of the hike he has to make every time his lettuces dry out.

For this reason many allotment gardeners store water in butts or in old galvanised tanks that can be purchased for a few pounds from scrap yards or plumbers. While this is very handy, it can be dangerous. Never sink such tanks level with the surface of the soil – small children might not notice them and no allotment holder wants to be responsible for the tragedy that might result. If you must store your water in such a container, make sure first of all that the Council approves of its installation, and secondly that it is raised clear of the ground. This is for safety reasons, to prevent rotting of the base, and to make emptying easier. Cover the top of the tank with plastic netting held in place by a brick at each corner. The netting is easy to remove when you want to dunk your can, and it will stop leaves and debris from fouling the water.

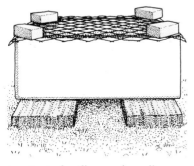

A water tank will save you endless tiring journeys across the allotments, but for safety's sake make sure it is covered with netting (which will also exclude leaves and other descending debris).

STORAGE

If the allotment is some distance from home, it can be a real bind lugging armfuls of tools to and from the plot every time you want to cultivate the soil. You can

either put up with this in the interests of getting a bit of exercise and secure in the know-ledge that your tools are safely under your care, or you can leave some or all of them at the allot-ment in a storage box or shed.

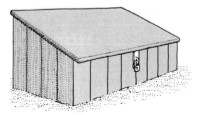

You don't need to be a master carpenter to knock up a toolbox, and it might prevent your fertilisers and tools from being stolen. Anchor the box to the ground with stakes, cover the lid with roofing felt and fit a stout padlock.

This is always risky, for however well made a shed or toolbox may be, and however securely it is anchored to the ground, there is always a chance that vandals will break and enter – especially on plots that cannot be seen from the road. A compromise might be the best solution. Leave bulky but cheaply replaced items such as a plastic watering can, garden line and bags of fertiliser and lime in the shed or box, but keep more pricey tools at home unless you can afford duplicate sets. A stout padlock and robust hinges will deter children who are out for a bit of mischief!

Bulky manure or compost is best stored in purpose-made bays at one end of the plot; if it is left in a heap it tends to spread over the plot and the path as well. Stout wooden posts treated with timber preservative should mark the corners of the bays (2m by 1.25m – 6ft by 4ft – is a convenient size) and the sides can be constructed of old floorboards or stout wire netting. Leave 1-cm (½-in) gaps between the floorboards to ensure air circulation. A removable front will make compost extraction easier. (For more details see page 21.)

ALLOTMENT PROBLEMS

The problems that face allotment owners rather than home gardeners occur mostly as a result of the plot not being under constant surveillance. In spite of widely publicised outbreaks of vandalism in which crops are up-rooted, sheds broken into and equipment stolen, this problem is a minor one in most areas. Far more likely is the loss of the occasional cabbage or cauliflower – especially from allotments adjacent to public footpaths and roads. There is only one way round this – grow enough crops to feed you and the pilferer, and site the crops you value most out of sight behind more mundane vegetables.

The only havoc ever wreaked on my own allotment was as a result of an overweight cow straying from the nearby field. She ate nothing but her feet made a real mess of my turnips! Check that the fences surrounding your allotment site are in good condition and inform the Council if they are not. It's their job (or the job of the neighbouring farmer) to keep boundaries in good repair. The other regular vandals you might encounter are birds, rabbits and deer, and they are dealt with fully in Chapter 10.

CONVERTING YOUR GARDEN

If you possess a large garden and want to turn part of it into an 'allotment' then most of this book will be just as relevant to you as it is to gardeners with a rented plot. The advantages of creating your own allotment are that you can govern its size, shape and proximity to the house and to water supplies. Make sure that the paths around the plot are wide enough to allow wheelbarrow access – 1.5m (5ft) is comfortable if you can spare it – and that there is provision for the storage of bulky soil enrichment like compost and manure.

3
TACKLING THE LAND

Every gardener taking on an allotment or vegetable plot feels that he's starting to do battle – especially if the ground is overgrown with weeds. If there is to be any chance of winning the first round then he must have a small but useful armoury of weapons that can cope with the untamed earth.

TOOLS

It's no use rushing out and buying a massive range of rather complicated implements until you know exactly which of them will be of any use, so content yourself with the following basic collection. Tools are not cheap, but if they are of good quality they will probably last as long as you will.

SPADE

Most likely the first tool you will need, this is also the one that has to take the most strain, so choose wisely. Look for a comfortable grip (in wood or polypropylene) and a close-grained shaft (which will be stronger) that is smoothly attached to the socket of the blade. The blade of a standard digging spade measures 29cm by 19cm (11½in by 7½in) and that of a lady's spade 25 cm by 16cm (10in by 6½in). Don't be too proud to select the smaller model if it feels more suited to your build. Weight and balance are the things to consider, and if you have sensitive skin, choose a 'YD' handle rather than the blister-making 'T' shape. Stainless steel spades (as opposed to those with forged steel blades) are very expensive and rather heavy in some cases but they are revered by many gardeners for working clay soil. **Uses** Digging, planting, skimming off weed growth.

FORK

There is no reason why the fork should not be used in the same way as the spade on heavy or stony earth; it makes digging a much easier task on these difficult soils. Look for the same features as the spade when it comes to handgrips and weight/balance. The prongs may be square in cross section or rather flattened in the case of the potato fork which was traditionally used for lifting this root crop. Either type is equally good for light soil cultivation. Again, there is a smaller border fork if you find the standard-sized model too large to handle easily. **Uses** Digging on heavy or stony soil, lighter cultivations, handling manure and compost, lifting vegetable crops, breaking down rough-dug soil.

RAKE

A smooth 1.5-m (5-ft) long handle in wood or tubular alloy and a 30-cm (12-in) long head fitted with 5-cm (2-in) teeth makes up the average rake. Make sure the handle is smooth and that the teeth are very solidly fitted to the head. **Uses** For levelling and breaking down soil and for raking up leaves, stones and the like. Beware of over-raking when you are preparing a seedbed or the soil will turn to dust which cakes in the first shower of rain.

DUTCH HOE

The most useful kind of hoe on my patch, this is the one with a flat blade attached to a 'horseshoe' of steel at the end of a 1.5-m (5-ft) handle. **Uses** For skimming off annual weed growth and for drawing drills against a garden line. The operator works backwards when weeding with this hoe

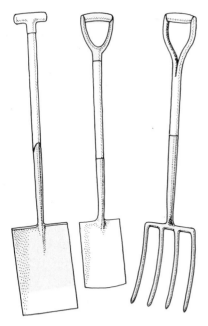

The gardener's armoury: (left) a digging spade and its smaller relation, the ladies' spade and a digging fork. Below: the flat-pronged potato fork, supposedly safer for lifting your spuds. Remember that 'YD' handles are less blister-making than the 'T' shape if your hands are tender. A garden line with metal spool and spike will last for ages. The Dutch hoe (far right) is an essential weeder and the draw hoe an optional earther-upper. The half-spoon cleaner shifts muck from them all.

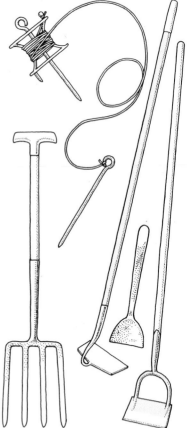

so the soil is left untrampled. Never hoe too deeply – the secret of successful hoeing is to sever annual weeds from their roots at ground level – not below.

TROWEL

This is the only stainless steel tool I possess! It is available in forged steel but is so much stronger and easier to use (and not prohibitively expensive) in stainless steel. Make sure that it has a comfortable and securely attached handle of close-grained wood. **Uses** Planting.

LINE

Whether you make one yourself or buy one, the garden line should be tough, non-stretch and free from knots which will instantly throw the blade of the drill-drawing hoe off course. Nylon or hemp cord is suitable and should be wound round a steel reel and spikes rather than wooden pegs which will rot and snap. **Uses** For drawing drills and generally marking out.

MEASURING ROD

This should be a 2-m or 6-ft length of 5 cm by 2.5cm (2in by 1in)

timber marked into metres and centimetres or feet and inches. Treat the timber with preservative to prolong its life, and make the marks with a saw rather than paint which may be masked by mud. **Uses** For planting out vegetables and fruit bushes.

SECATEURS

Choose the anvil type (with a blade that cuts against a flat surface) or the scissor type but make sure that the blades are of good quality and will respond to sharpening, either by you (preferably) or by the makers. Check that the secateurs are comfortable to use and not too large for your hand. **Uses** Essential for all pruning.

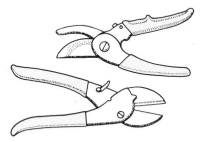

Choosing secateurs is a personal thing. The scissor type (above) and the anvil type (below) are both excellent provided they are kept sharp. Blunt secateurs are bad for the temper and for plants.

WATERING CAN OR HOSEPIPE

Galvanised cans are now so expensive that plastic (of a durable grade) is almost always a better buy. Hosepipes reinforced with nylon thread will last much longer than the cheaper types and are less likely to kink. **Uses** In spite of the rude remarks levelled at the British summer, you will need a watering can or hosepipe to make sure that crops do not dry out, especially in the early stages of growth.

ROTAVATOR

So often people think that the rotavator or garden cultivator (an electric or petrol-driven soil turning machine) is the answer to all soil cultivation problems. Unfortunately it creates quite a few problems of its own. Certainly it is very useful for breaking down land that has previously been cultivated but which is now fallow, so long as that land is not covered with *perennial* weeds. Annual weeds that have not seeded can be rotavated in with no compunction, but a rotavator used on ground that is infested with perennial weeds will simply chop them up and bury them – just what is needed to force them into renewed growth. The ground can be treated with a herbicide and then rotavated, but even then some weeds may escape and come through. Rotavate the soil too frequently at the same level and you are likely to cause a subsoil pan – an impenetrable barrier of hard ground that hinders drainage and root development. When you do decide that a rotavator would be useful (on fairly clean land that needs turning over quickly) make sure that the earth is well firmed afterwards as the rotavator will make it too light and fluffy for most vegetables. I'm not against the machine altogether; it's just that it must be used wisely.

MAINTENANCE AND CLEANING

Take care of your tools; they are not cheap to replace and will

The rotavator is not the answer to all cultivating problems but it is a great labour saver on land that has been previously cultivated. Firm the soil well with your feet after using one; it tends to fluff up the earth and leave too many air pockets – a sure way of getting loose-hearted cabbages and sprouts.

produce better results if they are looked after. Scrape off mud as soon as the job is done and rub over the metal parts with an oily rag to prevent rusting. The cutting edges of spades and hoes should be sharpened with a file from time to time to improve their keenness and make digging and hoeing easier.

A spade cleaner (for use during digging) can be made from an old spoon: cut off the top half of the bowl with a hacksaw and flatten the remainder with a hammer. Kept in your pocket, the half-spoon will be ready to skim the blade clear of sticking clay soil.

THE SOIL

Soils vary from place to place and the cultivation techniques needed to deal with them must vary also. These are the basic kinds of soil, one of which you are likely to find on your plot:

CLAY SOIL

Composed mainly of very fine particles which stick closely together, clay soils hang on to moisture which makes them very difficult to cultivate. In summer when they dry out they become rock hard and large cracks may appear in the surface. Clay soil is slow to warm up in spring. **Improve** matters by working in as much organic matter as possible so that the tiny clay particles clump together in larger groups. On acid clay soils annual liming will also help to improve the soil texture, but the results will not be so long lasting as when organic matter is incorporated. So-called clay cures (chemical applications) are limited in their efficacy. There is no substitute for the physical properties of compost and manure.

SANDY SOIL

This soil is light, easy to work, usually free-draining but inclined to dry out rapidly in summer. It also loses nutrients quickly.

Improve sandy soil by adding plenty of organic matter which will increase its fertility and moisture-holding capacity.

LOAM

This is the ideal soil but it exists in very few places! It is a combination of clay and sand, and probably silt, which drains well yet holds on to sufficient moisture to allow an even plant growth. Depending on the clay content, the loam may be described as heavy, medium or light.

SILTY SOIL

Not quite so sticky as clay because its particles are not so small, this is still inclined to be heavy and unworkable. When rubbed between the fingers it does not produce a surface quite so polished as a clay soil. **Improve** it exactly as for clay soil.

CHALKY SOIL

Soils containing a good deal of chalk are usually well-drained but still need plenty of organic matter to improve their fertility and lower their alkalinity. At high levels of alkalinity plants cannot extract certain essential nutrients. Vegetables often grow well on chalky soils.

STONY SOILS

These may either be of a sandy or chalky nature or have a high clay content. Whatever the situation, do not be tempted to remove barrowloads of stones – you will find that it is an endless job. Remove only the very largest and work around the rest. Over-raking will bring stones to the surface on any soil.

PEATY SOIL

High in organic matter, these soils are usually acid (sour) and poorly drained. **Improve** them by liming, applying coarse grit, sharp sand and weathered ashes. In severe cases, as with some clay soils, a drainage system may have to be constructed. (For more details on how to do this, see my *Gardening Techniques* volume in the *Royal*

Horticultural Society's Encyclopaedia of Practical Gardening listed in the Further reading section.)

SOIL ACIDITY

The amount of chalk or lime a soil contains governs its acidity and the plants which will grow in it. Soils containing a lot of lime are described as alkaline; those which lack lime are sour and described as acid.

Soil acidity is measured on the pH scale. This is rather a technical affair and I do not propose to go into it in detail, but every allotment gardener should know the pH level of his soil. He can then decide whether his earth needs lime to make the vegetables grow, or whether such an addition would only make matters worse. Very limy soils can be made more acid by applying organic matter and by using acidic fertilisers such as sulphate of ammonia rather than the alkaline fertilisers such as nitrochalk. Dusting the soil with flowers of sulphur is sometimes recommended but this is not long-lasting and has a limited effect.

The pH scale runs from 0 to 14, but only soils within the range 4.5 to 8.5 are common in Britain. Soils with lower readings are very acid and those with the higher readings very alkaline.

Simple kits with test tubes and solutions are now widely available to the gardener for testing the pH of his soil. Follow the instructions and test the various parts of your vegetable plot to see if the reading varies. Most vegetables enjoy a soil with a pH value of between 6.0 and 7.0. When you have tested your soil you can apply lime to raise its pH if it is too acid. Never apply lime at the same time as organic matter. A chemical reaction will be set up and much of the nitrogen (which plants need) will be lost. Apply the lime to the surface of the manured soil at least a month after the enrichment has been incorporated. Let the rains wash it in.

I always apply fertilisers in handfuls, but if you are adjusting the pH it is really better to apply the lime in precise quantities each winter. The table below shows how much lime is needed to raise the pH of a given soil to 6.5.

LAND CLEARANCE

Faced with a patch of weed-cloaked earth it's easy to be put off making a start, but if the job is tackled a bit at a time then it need not be so daunting. The best time to begin preparing your allotment is in autumn, for then you have a whole winter ahead of you during which to work the soil before sowings and plantings are to be made. Land left rough-dug (in large clods) through the winter will also be broken down by frost. This is not so important with sandy soils but very useful on heavy ground.

Start by clearing weed growth from the surface. Use your discretion and either skim it off with a spade, mow it (if it is grass), or tackle it with a bill-hook or sickle if it is really tough stuff.

HYDRATED LIME REQUIRED IN G (LBS) PER SQUARE METRE (YARD)

pH of soil	light sandy soil	peaty or clay soil	loamy soil
4.0	1.75kg (3¾lb)	2.25kg (5lb)	2kg (4½lb)
4.5	1.6kg (3lb)	1.9kg (4¼lb)	1.7kg (3½lb)
5.0	1kg (2¼lb)	1.65kg (3¼lb)	1.2kg (2¾lb)
5.5	675g (1½lb)	1kg (2¼lb)	900g (2lb)
6.0	340g (¾lb)	675g (1½lb)	450g (1lb)

Herbicides can be used as a last resort, but you'll still have to clear the dead growth after they have been applied (see Chapter 5 for herbicide recommendations).

The cleared debris can either be composted (if it will rot down) or burned (if it won't). If there is only a light covering of weed growth which is mainly of an annual nature, this can be thrown into the bottom of the trench during digging and no preliminary clearance will be necessary.

The order of events after the soil has been cleared is then as follows: dig and incorporate manure; allow the soil to settle and weather through the winter; apply lime if necessary; break down the soil with a fork two weeks before sowing or planting, incorporating fertilisers at the same time; rake level immediately before sowing.

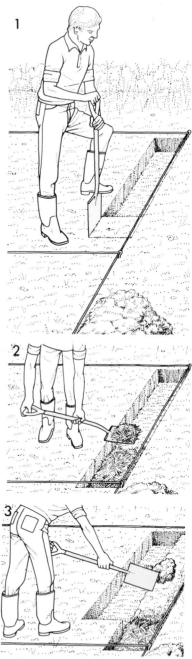

CULTIVATION TECHNIQUES

To make the best use of your tools and of your land it is important that you know how to carry out the basic soil cultivation techniques.

DIGGING

There are several methods of digging during which the soil is cultivated to different depths. In single digging the ground is worked to one spit (spade blade's depth) and during double digging it is worked to two spits. Trenching involves digging to three spits deep but is seldom practised nowadays except by masochistic gardeners. Few soils are deep enough to make trenching worthwhile.

SINGLE DIGGING METHOD

1 Divide the plot in two lengthways and take out a trench at the end of one half. The trench should be one spit deep and 30cm (12in) wide and the soil that is removed should be piled at the same end of the other half

of the plot. It will be used to fill the final trench.

2 Spread rotted manure or compost in the bottom of the trench if the soil is to be manured.

3 With the spade, cut and lift up

a spadeful of soil in front of the trench, and throw it forwards into the trench, flicking it upside-down so that weed growth is buried. Work sideways so that as another trench is opened, the soil from it is thrown into the first trench. Remove all perennial weed roots as the digging progresses. When a second trench has been created, manure can be spread in the bottom and the operation repeated. When one half of the plot has been dug, work back up the other half, filling the last trench with the soil that was removed from the first.

DOUBLE DIGGING METHOD

1 Take out a trench one spit deep and 60cm (2ft) wide and deposit the soil next to the site of the final trench (as for single digging).
2 Fork over the bottom of the trench to the full depth of the fork tines. Scatter manure over the bottom of the trench after this cultivation if you wish. Dig up and throw forward the soil in front of the trench in the same way as for single digging until a new 60-cm (2-ft) wide trench has been opened up
3 Repeat until the last trench is filled.

The line drawings should make both the single and the double digging operations easy to follow.

Remember that digging is a strenuous exercise. Always take it slowly until you are well used to the activity. Start by doing no more than half-an-hour a day, and do not take so much soil on your spade that it is difficult to lift. Never dig when the soil is so sticky that it clings to your spade and your wellies – it will put you off allotment gardening for life.

Having described double and single digging I ought to admit that soil which is already cultivated can be re-dug more easily. I have single-dug virgin soil to get rid of weed growth in the bottom of the trench, but I have seldom double dug except for examinations! It is really only worthwhile if you have a completely intractable subsoil that needs breaking up. Soil which is clean and relatively weed free can be dug or forked over without creating a trench. Simply lift and throw the soil forward, turning it over as you do so.

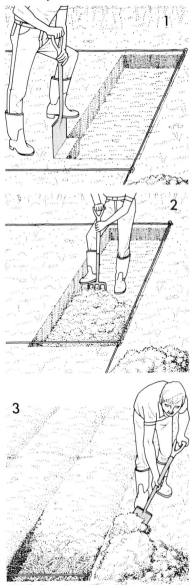

FORKING

Use the fork in place of the spade for digging when the soil is very heavy or stony. Otherwise use it to prick over the soil lightly to relieve compaction, to work in fertilisers, and as a sort of 'basher' to break down the clods of rough-dug soil in spring. Always use the back of the fork rather than the rake for breaking down soil prior to seed sowing. It brings fewer stones to the surface.

Get rid of your temper on a piece of rough-dug ground by breaking it down with the back of a fork – use it like a carpet beater. It brings fewer stones to the surface than a rake which can then be used simply for the final levelling.

HOEING

Use the Dutch hoe regularly to keep down weeds between the rows of crops. Work backwards using the tool in a 'push-pull' fashion so that the blade skims the surface of the soil and does not dig in too far. Held with its flat edge against a taut garden line so that one of its corners flicks away the soil, it can be used to take out seed drills (shallow grooves in the soil).

The draw hoe is not included on my list of essential tools but if you possess one already it can be used in a pulling motion to draw soil around crops when earthing up. It is also used for drawing drills and can be used to control weed growth in a chopping fashion. The

disadvantage is that the operator must work forwards so that he has to walk over the cultivated soil leaving an untidier finish than when a Dutch hoe is used.

Use a Dutch or push hoe to get rid of annual weed growth. Keep the hoe sharp and just skim it over the surface of the soil to part the weeds from their roots. The hoe won't be half so effective if you try to dig with it – keep those cultivations shallow.

The rake will produce the final level on your seedbed, but beware of over-raking or the surface will cake after the first shower of rain and you'll produce enough stones to build a rock garden.

RAKING

Too many people over-rake their soil. They push and pull this tool over the surface of the ground until all the stones have been found and the earth is dusty. The result is that the ground is far too fine for seed sowing and after the first shower of rain it cakes like cement. Use the fork to break down the soil and the rake to level it in long, sweeping motions.

COMPOST MAKING

This is a controversial matter – all keen gardeners have their own pet method. All I intend to do is to give you one system that works, then you can experiment yourself to see if you can make improvements.

Construct a strong bin to hold the compost. It should be 2.5m (8ft) long by 1.25m (4ft) wide and 1.25m (4ft) high, divided into two by a partition across the middle. Stout posts should mark the corners and the division and old floorboards or heavy gauge wire netting should form the sides and the partition. Make the front removable. This will give you two bins – one to be filling while the other is full and rotting. Line the sides of each bin with newspaper as it is filled to prevent the outer edges of the heap from drying.

Into the first bin place any rottable organic material: annual weeds, cabbage leaves, vegetable waste, tea leaves, crushed egg-shells, torn-up newspaper, lawn mowings, potato peelings, leaves and dead flowers. Do not compost waste food which will encourage rats, perennial weeds or woody stems, which will not rot down. Make sure that there is no concentration of any one item in any part of the bin as the mixture will rot down more speedily if well jumbled. Over every 23-cm (9-in) layer of material scatter a light dusting of sulphate of ammonia (a nitrogenous fertiliser which will speed up the rotting process) or a proprietary compost 'activator'.

Keep a piece of old carpet or sacking on top of the heap at all times to prevent excessive drying by sun and soaking by rain. If the heap looks dry at any time, soak it with a hosepipe and replace the carpet. When the bin is full, start to use the second one, leaving the first to rot down. Do not turn the compost – it's a waste of time. If properly constructed, the heap should rot down evenly and be ready to dig into the soil about six months after it was completed. Some folk claim to get quicker results than this, but I see little point in rushing nature – the stuff is easiest to use when brown and crumbly.

If you lack the minimal expert-

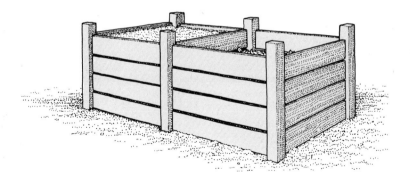

A pair of compost bins (one full and one filling) will help to keep you well supplied with organic enrichment. Stout posts and old floorboards (with gaps between) will make a sturdy bin.

Alternatively, heavy gauge wire netting may be used for the sides and partition if you prefer. Make the front removable and keep the top covered with a piece of old carpet or sacking.

ise needed to make a compost bin, then buy a proprietary one. Choose the biggest one possible, for you'll soon fill up a tiny container.

Whatever you make your compost in, do make good use of it. It's a free form of soil enrichment and improvement that no gardener can afford to be without. Worked into the earth in autumn at the rate of about one bucketful/sq m (sq yd) it will give a real boost to crops that are planted and sown in spring.

MANURE

Nice stuff if you can get it! If you know a friendly stable where you can obtain a trailer-load of manure for a modest fee then invest in it. Don't be tempted to dig in the material while it is fresh. Instead stack it for three months or so and dig it in when it has partially rotted down. Soil into which fresh manure has been dug is invariably short of nitrogen and produces spindly yellow plants. The shortage is due to the fact that the bacteria rob the soil of nitrogen as they break down the manure, so save them the trouble and your soil the nitrogen by rotting down the manure beforehand. **Apply** one bucketful/sq m (sq yd).

It's a good idea to give any manured soil a light dusting of sulphate of ammonia or nitrochalk in spring just to make sure that nitrogen is not lacking. Fourteen grams (½ oz) to the square metre (yard) should be enough.

As well as stable manure, you might also be able to lay in supplies of spent mushroom compost. This is a well-rotted material which contains manure plus a little chalk – a useful attribute where it is to be applied to acid soils. **Apply** half to one bucketful/sq m (sq yd).

Spent hops is a by-product of breweries. It smells a bit strong but makes a good soil conditioner.

Apply one bucketful/sq m (sq yd). Hop manure is spent hops plus fertilisers and has a lower application rate of four handfuls sq m (sq yd).

MULCHING

No gardener I know admits to having enough compost or manure to spare, but mulching – the spreading of a 5- or 8-cm (2- or 3-in) layer of well-rotted compost, manure or even leafmould alongside the plants – works wonders. It stops weeds from pushing through (or most of them at any rate) and it keeps in moisture, provided that it is laid when the ground is nicely dampened by rain. Dug in at the end of the season it helps to enrich and improve the soil.

Make sure that your mulches consist of well-rotted organic matter – fresh garden compost may still contain healthy weed seeds which germinate happily when spread on cultivated soil.

Strawberries and other crops such as potatoes can be mulched with black polythene. This adds no enrichment to the soil but it does suppress weeds and holds in moisture.

Remember that all mulches should be laid in spring on moist earth and dug in or removed

Black polythene makes a good weed-suppressing and moisture-retaining mulch around strawberries. Stretch it over the row in early June, make a hole above each plant and pull through the leaves and flowering stems.

during autumn. They prevent the heat gathered by the soil during the day from escaping at night, so if left in position in very cold weather, they can cause the crops immediately above them to be frosted.

FERTILISERS

Make no mistake about it – all soil needs both bulky enrichment in the form of organic matter and basic nutrients in the form of fertilisers. Plants need all sorts of minor elements if they are to survive but their three principal foods are nitrogen (N), phosphorous (P) and potassium or potash (K). Nitrogen generally stimulates leaf and shoot growth; phosphorous is valuable for root development and potassium aids flower and fruit production.

A general fertiliser contains equal parts of all three and you may see an analysis written on the side of the bag: 7:7:7. The elements are always given in the order N, P, K, so if you see a fertiliser with an analysis 7:7:14 you will know that it has double the amount of available potash and is therefore good for improving flower and fruiting qualities – tomatoes, capsicums and pumpkins will love it!

Fertilisers with a general action include Growmore (known through the war as National Growmore) and one which I confess to recommending frequently, blood, bone and fishmeal. This last-named fertiliser is organic; that is, it is derived direct from organic material and as well as imparting nutrients to the soil, it can also encourage soil bacterial activity which is vital to plant health. Inorganic fertilisers are 'man-made' and, although rich in certain plant nutrients, they are of no use to soil bacteria. (Remember that most bacteria in the soil are beneficial; only a few cause plant diseases.)

Some fertilisers offer one plant nutrient above all others, and these are useful for giving crops a boost in a given direction, whether it be the roots, shoots or fruits. The table on page 24 lists some of these fertilisers and their application rates as base dressings (applied to the soil before the crop is sown or planted) or top-dressings (applied when the crop is growing). I use both inorganic and organic fertilisers; some gardeners prefer to stick to those that are organically derived – the choice is up to you.

LIQUID FEEDS

Many growing crops appreciate liquid feeds which can get straight into the sapstream to give an instant boost. Many proprietary kinds are available, but I recommend a liquid tomato fertiliser for all fruit crops (such as strawberries, tomatoes, cucumbers and melons) and a general purpose liquid feed for leafy vegetables.

You can also make a liquid feed at home. Put some well-rotted manure into a sack and hang this in a water butt or tank. After a few weeks it will smell something awful but plants do seem to like it! Eight centimetres (3in) of the stuff in a can topped up with water will coax the most reluctant plants into growth.

Apply proprietary liquid feeds strictly in accordance with the manufacturer's instructions (don't add one for the can) and apply all liquid feeds when the soil is moist so that they can go straight into action.

Foliar feeds are useful for perking up green vegetables. They are diluted in water and sprayed on to the leaves from whence they are rapidly absorbed. Apply foliar feeds in dull weather (not bright sunshine) and check that you observe the regulation harvesting interval after spraying.

Fertiliser application rates

Fertiliser	Organic (O) or inorganic (I)	Quick (Q) or slow acting (S)	%N	%P	%K	Base dressing per sq. m (yd)	Top dressing per sq. m (yd)
Dried blood	O	Q	7–14	1–2	1	—	30–55g (1–2oz)
Steamed bone flour	O	S	1	27–28	—	55–110g (2–4oz)	—
Bone meal	O	S	3–5	20–25	—	55–110g (2–4oz)	—
Fishmeal	O	Q	8–10	5–10	1–2	85–110g (3–4oz)	—
Growmore	I	Q	7	7	7	55–110g (2–4oz)	55g (2oz)
Hoof and horn meal	O	Q (fine) S (coarse)	12–14	1–3	—	55–110g (2–4oz)	—
John Innes Base	I	Q	5.1	7.2	9.7	55–110g (2–4oz)	—
Nitrate of potash	I	Q	12–14	—	44–46	—	14–30g ($\frac{1}{2}$–1oz)
Nitrate of soda	I	Q	16	—	—	—	14–30g ($\frac{1}{2}$–1oz)
Nitro-chalk	I	Q	15.5	—	—	30g (1oz)	30g (1oz)
Sulphate of ammonia	I	Q	20–21	—	—	30–55g (1–2oz)	30g (1oz)
Sulphate of potash	I	Q	—	—	48	14–30g ($\frac{1}{2}$–1oz)	14–30g ($\frac{1}{2}$–1oz)
Superphosphate	I	S	—	18.5	—	30–55g (1–2oz)	—
Triple Superphosphate	I	S	—	47	—	10–21 ($\frac{1}{3}$–$\frac{3}{4}$oz)	—
Urea	O	Q	46	—	—	—	14–30g ($\frac{1}{2}$–1oz)

4
GROWING SYSTEMS

To get the best out of your land you'll have to master a few skills and, above all, plan which crops are to be grown where and when. There are many techniques that can be learned in allotment gardening, but those discussed below are some of the most important.

SEED SOWING

The vast majority of fruit and vegetable seeds are sown direct into the ground where they are to grow. This is known as direct drilling, the seeds being placed in shallow grooves or 'drills' made across the plot.

Before you sow any seeds in this fashion, make sure that the soil is in a fit state to take them. It wants to be moist, but not so sticky that it clings to your boots and implements. Try to sow in a mild spell, rather than a cold snap. The soil should be well cultivated – dug or forked over, enriched if necessary, broken down, raked level and allowed to settle for a few days.

To sow in drills, first stretch the garden line across the raked soil to mark the exact position of the row making sure it is taut by pushing the pegs in as you stretch the line. Take up your Dutch or draw hoe and stand with both feet on the line (see diagram). With slow, gentle movements, pull the hoe along the line so that it takes out a drill of the required depth. Shuffle backwards as the drill is opened up, keeping your feet on the line so that it doesn't move.

When the drill is drawn, label the row to show the variety being sown, then mark either end with a stout cane or stick. Remove the line so that it does not get in the way of sowing.

Sow all seeds thinly so that they rest at least 0.5cm (¼in) apart. Sown too close they will fight for space and may fall prey to fungus diseases. Larger seeds can be space sown to cut down the need for thinning later on. If the plants are to be spaced 15cm (6in) apart when they are mature, then sow at 8cm (3in) intervals and remove every other plant (if every seed germinates!).

Seed dressings are useful for early sowings. They are powders which contain a fungicide and they can be dropped into the packet of seeds and shaken up to give each one a protective coating. This treatment is particularly useful with early-sown peas and broad beans.

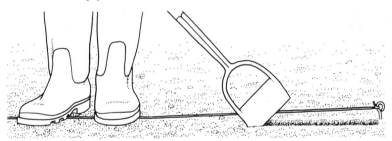

The Dutch hoe makes a handy drill-drawer. Stand on the line to keep it taut and gently pull away the soil to make a shallow furrow.

When the seeds are sown, carefully pull back the soil with a rake so that the drill is re-filled. There should be no need to water if the soil is moist, but keep an eye on it from now onwards and turn a sprinkler on (or use a can fitted with a sprinkler head) if it shows signs of drying out.

SEEDBEDS

Plants such as cabbages, cauliflowers and other brassicas (members of the cabbage family) are seldom sown where they are to grow. This is because they take a relatively long time to mature and the land can be utilised for other crops while the brassicas

On heavy ground a raised seedbed supported by wooden boards is especially useful – the seeds can be sown in close-spaced drills and will get away to a good start in the well-prepared soil.

are young. If sown on a seedbed there is also less wastage, for the young plants that grow can nearly all be used.

Choose the site of your seedbed with care. The spot should be sheltered from winds, in full sun and on soil which is well-drained. If the land is not well drained then build a seedbed which is raised up from the soil within 23cm (9in) wooden boards. A bed 1m (3ft) wide running across one end of the plot is often a convenient arrangement.

The seedbed should be well prepared each autumn. Dig it over and work in peat, leafmould and even grit if the soil is on the heavy side. Don't add manure or compost which may produce sappy growth in the early days of development. Break down the soil with a fork in spring and then leave it for two weeks before sowing. Rake the surface level when you are ready to sow and rake in a couple of handfuls of bonemeal to each square metre (yard). Sow the seeds in drills (just as you would on the vegetable plot) but space the rows much closer together as the plants will be removed by the time they are a few centimetres high.

THINNING

With most crops, the earlier the seedlings are thinned the better. This prevents the chosen plants from becoming starved and

Thin all seedlings as soon as they are large enough to handle. It seems wasteful, but the job has to be done quickly if the remaining plants are to produce the best crops.

spindly due to competition for nutrients and light. Try to thin when the soil is moist (immediately after a shower is ideal). Hold the soil around the seedlings that are to be retained with one hand and pull up the unlucky ones with the other. Instead of thinning once to the final spacing, try to thin twice so that any plants which are later polished off by slugs or birds can be replaced.

TRANSPLANTING AND PLANTING

Both these jobs are best done

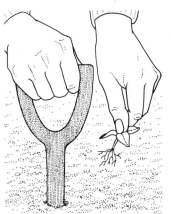

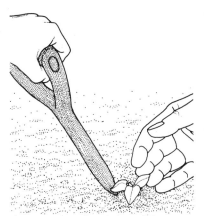

A stout dibber (made from a broken spade handle) makes an effective planting tool for many vegetables, especially brassicas. Make a hole for the youngster, drop it in and then push the soil firmly back against the roots.

when the soil is moist but not wet. Soak the seedbed a day before transplanting, if that's where the plants are being moved from, and lift them the following day with a trowel, discarding any that are weak and feeble. Replant with a trowel, usually to the same level at which the plant was growing in the seedbed, firming the soil thoroughly around the roots. Brassicas are often planted with a dibber – a pointed stick which is first used to poke a hole in the soil and, after the plant's roots are inserted, to poke back the earth around them.

Give all plants a thorough watering-in after planting so that their roots are settled into contact with the soil. Remember that the days immediately after transplanting are probably the riskiest in the plant's life, so look after your charges and don't let them get thirsty.

DEEP BED CULTIVATION

A system developed relatively recently, this method of growing vegetables has found favour with a lot of gardeners. I've never used it so cannot offer first-hand advice on its efficacy, but friends who have tried the method speak very highly of it. Briefly the system is this: the vegetables are grown in beds of soil 1 to 1.25m (3 to 4ft) wide running across the plot with paths left between the beds for access. In the first year, when the beds are prepared they are double dug (see page 19) and enriched with plenty of well-rotted manure or garden compost. Crops are later sown and planted as normal but the soil is never walked on – all cultivations are carried out from the paths. The crops can be grown closer together and reputedly give a generous harvest. In subsequent winters more organic matter is forked or dug in (if the crops need it) but after this the beds are not trampled at all. The soil remains light and airy at all times.

NO-DIG SYSTEM

This ought to appeal to any lazy gardener! Once the soil has been initially cleaned and cultivated no further disturbance is allowed. Instead the surface of the soil is covered with a 5- to 8-cm (2- or 3-in) layer of well-rotted compost or manure which retains the moisture, keeps down weeds and is mixed into the soil by the worms. More mulches are applied through the growing season. The argument for this kind of cultivation is that routine soil cultivation disturbs the good works of earthworms and bacteria, while the mulch system encourages their activity.

On the debit side it cannot be denied that copious supplies of organic matter are necessary to keep the land in good heart, and I have seen some pretty poor root crops grown on land that has not been dug for several years. The compaction caused by rains and also by feet (if the land is walked on) stunts and distorts the otherwise long and slender roots of carrots, parsnips and the like.

ORGANIC GROWING

I hesitate to embark on a discussion as to the merits of organic gardening. It's a personal matter and you must decide for yourself whether or not you will use inorganic fertilisers or those which are derived from natural carbon-containing materials. I use both. The organic kinds keep the soil healthy by encouraging bacterial activity as well as plant growth, but they are often slower acting than the inorganic 'man-made' fertilisers which are valuable for giving crops a boost (see the chart on page 24).

Sadly gardeners who admit to not being 'organic' in their outlook will often be accused of being irresponsible, but the fact that they use artificial fertilisers does not mean that they are also trigger-happy when it comes to spraying chemicals around. The sensible gardener will keep his soil in good heart by working in plenty of 'bulky organics' to improve its structure and workability, and by applying the right fertiliser at the right time. Inorganic fertilisers should certainly be applied with care, for some of them are very strong and may affect the flavour of certain crops if applied at the wrong time. Where their use is necessary I have indicated application rates for the individual vegetables and fruits.

CATCH-CROPPING

A natty little trick for making sure you get the most out of your limited space. Quick-growing crops like radishes, lettuces and spring onions are grown on land that will later be occupied by other crops such as brassicas. By the time the brassicas are ready for planting out, the quicker-maturing crop will have been harvested and your season will have been enriched as a result.

INTERCROPPING

Again the quick-maturing crops are used and this time sown between rows of larger plants which, when they are fully grown, will need all the space. The radishes or whatever will have plumped up and been picked before the leaves of the big boys on either side have encroached too much on the inter-row space.

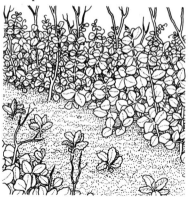

Intercropping is a clever way of getting the maximum yield from your allotment space.

CROPPING PLANS

Every winter when you make out your seed order, draw up a plan of the crop arrangement on your allotment. You will then be able to calculate approximately how much seed you will need of which varieties of vegetable. Crops that like manure can be grouped together, as can those for which the ground needs liming, and you can work out the times at which the ground will be occupied by each crop. The cropping plan you draw up will obviously reflect your taste in vegetables, but the layout on page 36 will give you some ideas. Try to plan for a succession of crops (rather than gluts), and grow also those crops which are likely to be expensive in the shops – particularly the case with winter-harvested vegetables such as leeks, broccoli and Brussels sprouts in hard winters.

SUCCESSIONAL SOWING
Many crops mature quite quickly and it is far better to sow short rows at intervals of a few weeks to give a continuous harvest rather than one useless glut.
Recommended sowing intervals are indicated where necessary in the A-Z of Vegetables and Herbs sections.

CROP ROTATION
Most gardening writers are guilty of assuming that gardeners can work the same kind of rotation systems as can farmers. Whilst this is obviously not true, because gardening is on a smaller scale, the basic principles are sound. Grow your crops in a different spot each year so that they are less likely to fall foul of specific pests and diseases, and so that the soil is not robbed of the same nutrients season after season.

Some gardeners insist on growing crops like onions in the same highly enriched soil every year. It's a chance they are prepared to take, but if disease does get into that bed (in the form of white rot) then it means that onions cannot be grown on the infected soil for a good number of years.

For convenience it is possible to group crops together in a crop rotation scheme and to move them all from one part of the plot to another the following year. Those which enjoy plenty of manure in the soil (such as peas, beans, celery, leeks and onions) are grown together, as are those which prefer ground that was manured for a previous crop

(carrots and most root crops). Others (brassicas) like a soil which has been limed and they, too, can be grouped.

CROPS UNDER COVER
In the garden the greenhouse is the most important structure when it comes to growing crops under cover. On the allotment the likelihood of vandalism, the temporary nature of renting, and maybe even Council regulations, will mean that some alternative form of cover must be sought.

There are two types of structure which the allotment gardener has at his disposal: the frame and the cloche.

FRAMES
Although they are less portable than cloches, frames are a good investment where early crops are to be grown, where seedlings are to be raised and where melons, capsicums and cucumbers are grown regularly. Buy a proprietary frame or build your own from old floorboards (or bricks) and a redundant window frame (see diagrams). Alternatively, glaze your 'box' with thick polythene sheeting. Whatever materials you use remember that you are aiming for a combination

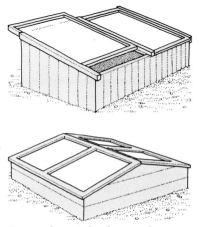

You can buy garden frames: the single-span is shown above and the double-span below.

29

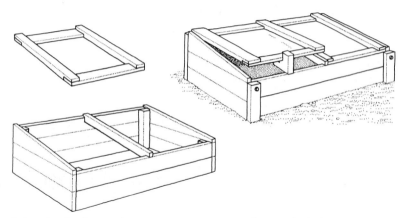

It is quite simple to make your own frames using old floorboards and assorted timber. The 'lights' can be glazed or polythene covered and the structure anchored to the ground with stout stakes to which the sides of the frame are bolted. A stepped wooden block makes an adjustable prop for the lights.

of good insulation and maximum light transmission.

Frames may be of two types. Single-span frames are equipped with a sloping 'light' which is best positioned so that it faces south. Double-span frames have a central ridge and can run in any direction. If you build a frame yourself make sure that it is deep enough to accommodate the plants you want to grow. Make it 30cm (1ft) deep at the back and 23cm (9in) deep at the front if you want to use it solely for raising early salads and seedlings. If melons, cucumbers and capsicums are to be grown inside it, then it should be at least 30cm (1ft) deep at the front, rising to 45cm (1½ft) at the rear. As with cloches, glass gives better light transmission and retains heat longer than polythene; it also has a longer life. Although it will be more expensive at the outset, a frame made from glass and timber or brick will last indefinitely.

Site the frame where it will be easily accessible from the path. Anchor it well to the ground with wooden posts to which the sides of the frame are screwed or bolted. Make sure the posts and any wooden parts of the frame are treated with a timber preservative such as Cuprinol (which is based on copper naphthenate). Do not use creosote which gives off fumes that are poisonous to plants. Make sure that the frame is on firm and level ground so that the light sits comfortably in place.

The frame should be positioned in a spot that receives excellent light but not on low-lying ground where frost and cold air collects. Prepare and enrich the soil within the frame as described for the crop being grown or as recommended for seedbed construction (see page 26).

On the allotment, heating is generally out of the question, but in the garden (where electricity is available) proprietary soil-warming cables can be laid in the soil to raise its temperature in spring and make an earlier start possible. These specially manufactured cables are armoured for safety and can be snaked across the bottom of the frame 10cm (4in) below soil level. If a rod-type thermostat is connected to the system and fitted to the inside of the frame, the temperature can be controlled and money saved.

On cold spring nights the frame

will need insulating. Cover it with old carpeting, sacks or straw bales if these are available. Tie down the light with stout cord or wire when heavy winds blow to keep it in place.

Ventilate the frame whenever the sun shines and the weather is relatively mild. Some proprietary frames are equipped with adjustable casement stays; home-made frames can be provided with a stepped wooden block so that the front of the light can be wedged open to a chosen degree. Shading will be necessary in summer and for this you can use any of the proprietary 'washes' that are available, or (more expensive) plastic blinds. I find that closeweave green plastic netting is a cheap compromise between messy whitewash and pricey blinds. Fasten it to wooden frames with drawing pins; to aluminium frames with ingenuity or Blu-tack.

Water frame-grown plants carefully, always taking care to water the soil and not the plant foliage. Semi-automatic watering can be achieved if you lay a length

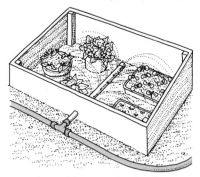

A perforated hose or plastic tube makes a good semi-automatic watering device for a garden frame. When the hosepipe is turned on, the plants are gently watered via small perforations in the pipe.

of perforated hosepipe among the plants and connect this to the allotment tap whenever you want to water. This system at least

makes sure that the water gets where it is wanted and it saves you from impersonating Gunga-din with a watering can.

As well as for raising seedlings, the frame can also be used to harden them off prior to planting out. Give them more and more ventilation until they are used to the temperatures in the world outside. Early crops of carrots, lettuces, radishes and the like can also be cultivated when the soil outdoors is cold and inhospitable (see individual crops for recommendations).

CLOCHES

A vegetable gardener who doesn't use cloches is only firing on two cylinders. They really do open up a new world of growing and should be part of every allotment holder's armoury.

The word cloche (pronounced to rhyme with gosh and not with gauche) is the French word for bell. It was originally applied to 'bell jars', those glass domes that covered tender plants in Victorian kitchen gardens. Today bell jars are collector's items, but the new cloches – shaped like tents, tunnels or barns – are enjoying increased popularity. The classic glass cloche with sides and roof panels (rather like a miniature greenhouse) was developed by Major Chase in 1912. The wire supports are now manufactured by the firm of Picken & Sons Ltd., (see page 152). No one else makes them (you'll have to supply the glass yourself).

Other excellent cloches include the Westray type (barn or tent shape) which has removable roof panes. Beneath these the cloche is covered with strong black netting to repel birds – a useful feature where pigeons and sparrows are a problem.

Many plastic tunnel cloches are now available and they are often made from materials which have a life expectancy of between five

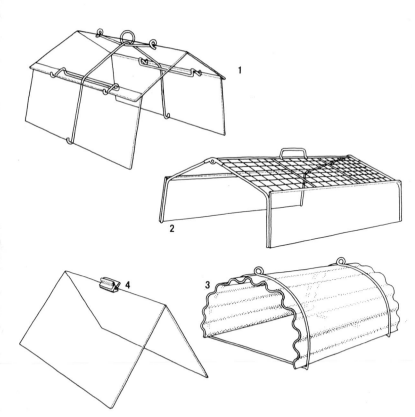

There are many different types of cloche on the market today, but among the best are the original Chase barn type (1); the Westray cloche (2) with its covering of plastic net which repels birds once the glass has been removed; an ICI Novolux cloche (3) made of long-lasting corrugated plastic; and a glass tent cloche (4) held together with a Rumsey clip.

and 15 years. Polythene and some of the flimsier plastics will only last for two or three years before they are made brittle by exposure to sunlight. Glass cloches will last indefinitely if they are taken care of and not clouted by a misrouted wheelbarrow, but they are heavy, dangerous to children and costly at the outset. Plastic cloches will not retain heat so efficiently as glass ones, but they are lighter, more easily portable and often cheaper. Mind you, they blow away more easily too! (See pages 152-3 for names and addresses of suppliers.)

When buying any cloche look for strength, good light transmission, portability, durability, and ease of ventilation. Choose the cheaper and smaller tent and tunnel cloches for low-growing crops and barn cloches for heftier vegetables. Polythene tunnels can be made at home from stout wire hoops, nylon twine and long sheets of polythene. They are the cheapest form of cover and can be recommended, but do bear in mind that you will have to replace the polythene every two years. (See the diagrams on page 33 for construction.)

The advantage of cloches of any type is that they protect the plants from wind, prevent the soil from being repeatedly soaked by freezing rain and reduce the likelihood of frost damage. Put in place at least two weeks before the crop is sown or planted, they will let the soil dry out a little, so raising its temperature a fraction and making conditions more amenable to plant growth. Don't think of them as steaming hothouses, think of them as umbrellas and windbreaks that will allow you to make an early start to the season and prolong its bounty at the other end as well.

Prepare the soil for the crop before you position the cloches, and make sure that they are firmly bedded on level ground. Anchor them with pegs and stout twine if necessary. Sit them as close together as possible and fix endpieces firmly in place to prevent the row from acting as a wind

tunnel. The longer you can leave them in position before the crop is sown or planted the better.

As the crops grow, watering and ventilation will become important. Unless the plants are very small (when direct watering of the soil will be necessary) all water can be applied over the top of the cloches. It will run off the glass and move downwards *and sideways* to reach the plant roots. This saves you the arm-aching chore of lifting up the cloches every time you want to water.

Many cloches have facilities for ventilation – either panes which can be propped open on special wires, or sliding side panels in the case of some plastic tunnels. Those which cannot be adjusted to allow in air must be propped up on bricks or flowerpots. On very

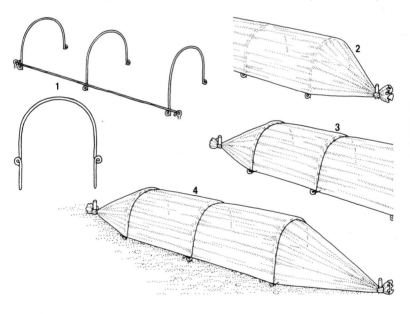

Plastic tunnel cloches are easy to make. Position a garden line where the tunnel is to run and push in stout wire hoops equipped with loops twisted into them 15cm (6in) above the base of each leg. When the hoops are pushed into the ground the loops should rest on the surface (1). Stretch polythene along the row and over the hoops, **anchoring it at either end by tying it to a stake (2). Link the two loops on each hoop with a piece of nylon twine to hold the polythene in place while still allowing it to be lifted for ventilation and crop examination (3). Bury the edges in the soil to exclude draughts (4).**

warm days, every other cloche can be removed to allow the plants a good breather.

Shading is seldom necessary, for when the sun shines so brightly then the cloches can be removed completely. It is at removing time that you will appreciate the cloches which have handles, for this makes the task much easier. Remember to harden off any cloched crop by increasing ventilation each day before the protection is completely removed.

Store the cloches with care. Many of them will sit neatly inside one another and can be stored on their ends out of the way in a shed or garage. Others will fold flat.

As well as starting crops early, don't forget that cloches are useful for ripening crops such as onions before they are stored in the

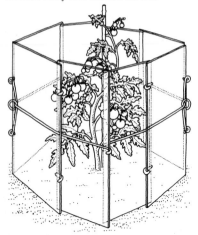

Two barn cloches stood on end around a tomato plant will protect it from winds and hasten fruit ripening. Canes or twine can be used to hold the cloches firm.

autumn. Two barn cloches stood on end around individual tomato plants will keep them happy in summers that are less than baking.

Recommendations for cloche growing are included under the individual crop headings; specific cloche cropping programmes are given on pages 35-7. The following crops are recommended where continuous cloche or frame cover can be provided, though in the heart of summer a few of them can be grown uncovered in milder parts of the country: aubergine, capsicum, endive, cucumber and melon. (See Chapters 6 and 8.)

CROPPING PLAN FOR YEAR-ROUND VEGETABLES

The plan on pages 36-7 offers a suggestion, nothing more, on how an allotment can be planned to yield a varied harvest right through the year. If the plot runs north/south then the top end of the plan should taken as the north end. If the plot runs east/west then the left-hand side should be taken as the north side. Any crop that you prefer not to grow can simply be ignored on the plan and the next crop shunted forward.

Those parts of the plot that are enclosed in a brown line should be manured in the winter before sowing or planting. Those which are not in a brown bordered area should be grown on land that has been enriched with fertiliser rather than manure.

Remember that crops should be moved around each year to prevent soil sickness and a build-up of specific pests and diseases.

Cloche cropping programme

The continuous line indicates when the cloches are in position. The arrow shows the sowing or planting time.
By switching the cloches from one crop to another through the season they can be put to maximum use.
(Where a specific variety has been given, this is because it is suitable for that particular time of year.)

Jan	Feb	Mar	Apr	May	Jun	Jul	Aug	Sep	Oct	Nov	Dec
Peas – Feltham First											
	Turnip										
			Tomatoes								
Lettuce (cont)				French bean							
		Strawberries							Radish		
					Melons	Capsicums					
Peas (cont)			Runner bean								
				Courgettes/Marrows							
Broad bean (cont)											
				Sweet corn					Lettuce – Kwiek		
	Potatoes – Harbinger								Lettuce – Imperial Winter		
		Carrots							Peas – Meteor		
									Broad bean – The Sutton		

35

Cropping plan for year-round vegetables

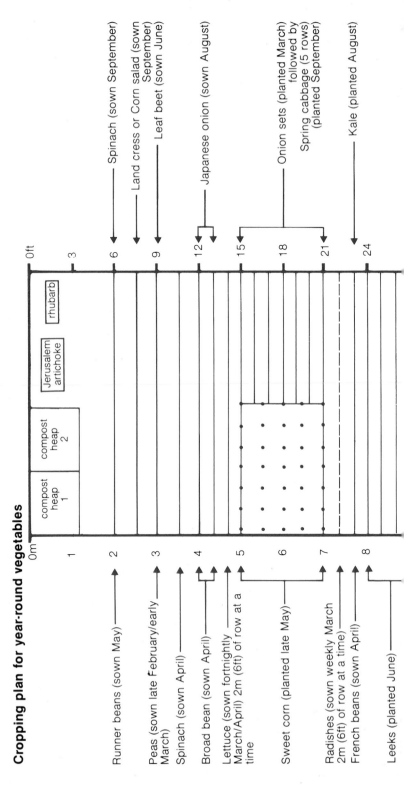

0m
1
2 — Runner beans (sown May)
3 — Peas (sown late February/early March)
— Spinach (sown April)
4 — Broad bean (sown April)
5 — Lettuce (sown fortnightly March/April) 2m (6ft) of row at a time
6 — Sweet corn (planted late May)
7 — Radishes (sown weekly March 2m (6ft) of row at a time)
— French beans (sown April)
8 — Leeks (planted June)

compost heap 1
compost heap 2
Jerusalem artichoke
rhubarb

0ft
3
6 — Spinach (sown September)
— Land cress or Corn salad (sown September)
9 — Leaf beet (sown June)
12 — Japanese onion (sown August)
15 — Onion sets (planted March) followed by Spring cabbage (5 rows) (planted September)
18
21
24 — Kale (planted August)

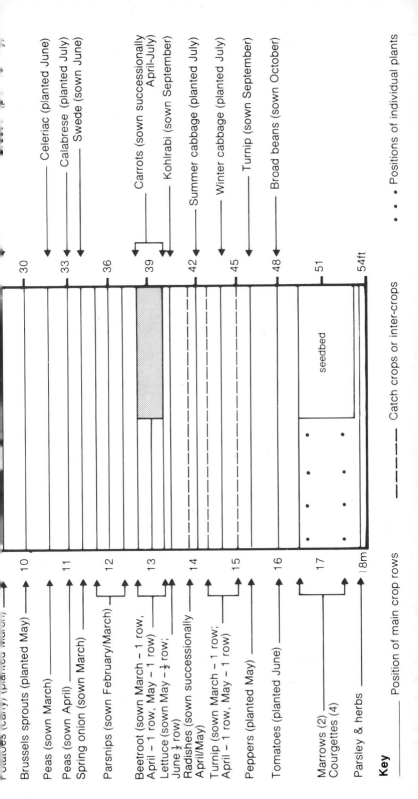

Potatoes (early) (planted March)
Brussels sprouts (planted May) —— 10
Peas (sown March)
Peas (sown April) —— 11
Spring onion (sown March)
Parsnips (sown February/March) —— 12
Beetroot (sown March – 1 row,
April – 1 row, May – 1 row)
Lettuce (sown May – ½ row;
June ½ row) —— 13
Radishes (sown successionally
April/May) —— 14
Turnip (sown March – 1 row;
April – 1 row, May – 1 row) —— 15
Peppers (planted May)
Tomatoes (planted June) —— 16
Marrows (2) —— 17
Courgettes (4)
Parsley & herbs —— 18m

Celeriac (planted June)
Calabrese (planted July) —— 30
Swede (sown June) —— 33
—— 36
Carrots (sown successionally
April-July)
Kohlrabi (sown September) —— 39
Summer cabbage (planted July) —— 42
Winter cabbage (planted July) —— 45
Turnip (sown September)
Broad beans (sown October) —— 48
—— 51
—— 54ft

seedbed

Key

—— Position of main crop rows

------ Catch crops or inter-crops

• • • Positions of individual plants

37

5 WEED CONTROL

There's no getting away from it; weeds on the vegetable plot have to be controlled if the cultivated crops are to produce a decent harvest. Not only do the weeds compete with the vegetables for light, water and nutrients, but they also harbour pests and diseases which they are quite happy to pass on to their more legitimate bedfellows.

There are two distinct kinds of weed: those which are annual (growing from seed, flowering, setting seed and dying within the space of a year) and those which are perennial (overwintering usually by means of a thick root system and re-emerging year after year). Both types of weed are a pain in the neck but perennials are the most difficult to shift.

Of the annuals, groundsel, chickweed, shepherd's purse and hairy bittercress are perhaps the most common. They are easy to bump off but should nevertheless be attended to before they set seed, or the old adage 'one year's seed; seven years' weed' will seem particularly apt.

Perennial weeds cling on to life and to the ground with great tenacity. Couch grass, bindweed, ground elder, marestail, creeping buttercup and (probably worst of all) oxalis, have sent many gardeners indoors under a black cloud. Dandelion, dock, nettles, Japanese knotweed and thistles can also amount to a plague, but if the soil is purged of all these roots at the time of the first soil clearance, then subsequent cultivations should provide all the discouragement necessary.

MECHANICAL WEED CONTROL
Under this heading I include hand weeding - not the most popular garden chore but certainly one of

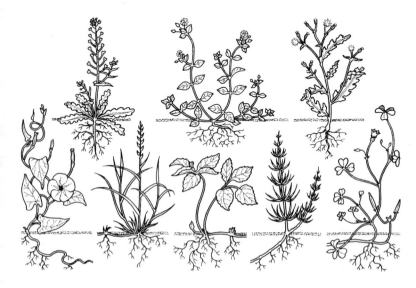

Unfortunately weeds on the allotment are a fact of life. Some of those you will encounter are (from top left): shepherd's purse, chickweed, groundsel, bindweed, couch grass, ground elder, marestail and oxalis.

the most effective. Among the plants within the row it is by far the safest method of weed control and it does help you to get to know your plants and to see how they are developing. Annual weeds are easy and satisfying to pull up by hand; deeper-rooted perennials such as dandelions, thistles and docks can be levered out with a trowel.

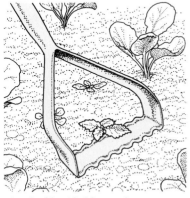

This double-sided hoe makes every stroke a working one, and the hollow-ground blade is self-sharpening.

Between the rows there is nothing better for rapid weed clearance than a Dutch hoe or a double-sided hoe. Keep in mind that the object of hoeing is to separate the upper part of the weed from its root system. Skim the blade across the surface of the soil or fractionally below it but do not push it too deeply. Too many gardeners try to dig with a hoe and the weeds survive as a result. In dry weather the severed weed growth can be left on the surface of the soil to dry out. Sharpen your Dutch hoe occasionally with a file - you'll find that it's much easier to use than one which has been blunted through years of use.

Hoeing is really only effective against annual weeds – perennials will simply sprout again from their root system if cut off at their stocking tops. Dig them out with a trowel if they are present in small numbers, or go in between the rows with a fork if they are greatly in evidence.

Thorough soil cultivation in winter is the most reliable method of eliminating the majority of perennial weeds. Keep your eyes on the soil as you turn it and pull out any thick roots, taking care not to break off even the tiniest section which will be happy to take on a life of its own. Annual weeds can be composted, and although some gardeners claim that their heap is hot enough (it will heat up due to bacterial action) even to kill off perennial weed roots, I would not risk composting these. Instead put them in a pile in one corner so that they can either be left to rot down for a year or more or burned on the annual bonfire.

CHEMICAL WEED CONTROL

I am not a fan of weedkillers in the garden, least of all on the vegetable plot. They have a habit of spreading where they are not wanted and of killing off the vegetables as well as the weeds. Good cultivation, both in winter when the ground is clear and in summer when the crops are growing, will be all the control needed to keep these plant aliens in check, but for those who are so short of time that they have to kill off weeds by using herbicides (the scientific name for weedkillers), then I offer the following advice:

1 Observe all the safety precautions indicated by the manufacturer and use and store the product with great care.
2 Use the right product for the job.
3 Use the product on a still day and keep all pets and children indoors while you are applying the solution and off the area until the following day at least.
4 Do not use a sprayer for weed control – use a watering can fitted with a dribble bar or a sprinkler head so that there is no danger of 'spray drift'.

Some herbicides have to be sprayed on to weed foliage; applying others with a watering can and dribble bar avoids spray drift.

5 Keep a can and dribble bar specifically for weed control and label it as such. This prevents other plants from being affected by residues.

6 Don't mix more solution than you need. Flush any surplus solution down the lavatory.

7 Wear old clothes and rubber gloves when you spray and mix solutions outdoors.

8 Wash thoroughly after using weedkillers and keep any equipment and products out of reach of children and animals.

9 Buy weedkillers in small quantities which you can use within one year of purchase.

TYPES OF WEEDKILLER

There are several kinds of weedkiller which act in different ways. Those which are **selective** in their action will kill only certain types of weed. (Lawn weedkillers are selective for example because they don't kill grass.) Other herbicides are **total** weedkillers and kill any green plant. **Contact** weedkillers will kill only that green material with which they come into contact. **Translocated** weedkillers, however, may only touch one leaf of a plant but they are taken into the sapstream and

moved round the entire plant, thus bringing about its demise. (They are also known as **systemic** weedkillers.) **Residual** weedkillers are usually watered onto clean ground where they will form a barrier that cannot be penetrated by weeds; they are particularly useful on paths and rose beds where they can keep the soil clean for up to a year.

WHICH WEEDKILLER FOR WHICH WEED?

For clearing ground of weeds prior to cultivation, use a weedkiller containing glyphosate. This is effective against a wide range of annual and perennial weeds but it does not persist in the soil.

For killing off surface growth of perennial weeds and totally killing annual weeds use a weedkiller containing paraquat and diquat.

For killing off woody weeds such as brambles use a weedkiller containing 2,4,5-T or ammonium sulphamate.

For killing off couch grass use a weedkiller containing dalapon.

To keep ground around soft fruit bushes clear of weeds use a weedkiller containing simazine.

For killing difficult weeds such as oxalis, ground elder and bindweed, use repeated applications of a weedkiller containing glyphosate.

SODIUM CHLORATE

This total weedkiller has been sold for many years by most ironmongers and garden shops. It is most effective at killing all plant life but it is not a herbicide I would recommend. It is highly inflammable (though it is now available treated with a fire depressant), and it moves sideways in the soil as well as downwards – often killing the plants in adjacent beds and borders. It is active in the soil for at least six months, so crops cannot be planted or sown for at least half a year after application. It also corrodes metal, and must be applied with a plastic can and sprinkler bar.

6
A-Z OF VEGETABLES

Vegetables naturally take up most of the space on any allotment and when grown from seed they offer staggering value for money. But don't just stick to potatoes, cabbages and carrots – do go out of your way to try one or two new kinds each year to widen your skills and titillate your palate.

Vegetables, more than anything else, respond to watering and feeding. Most of them thrive on a relatively rich diet and need to be grown quickly so that they are tender and juicy. Crops that have had to struggle for light, moisture and food will invariably have the flavour and tenderness of solid mahogany.

Read Chapter 4 before you grow your vegetables, so that you can plan what goes where and when it will crop. I have marked each crop of vegetables and fruit (Chapter 8) with stars to indicate how much effort I think is needed to grow it well. The greater the number of stars, the more fiddly and time-consuming the crop is to grow. Idlers should stick to the one-star ratings!

Where relevant at the end of most entries I have included brief notes on growing for showing. Most flower shows give prizes to vegetables that are grown well, exhibiting the crop to perfection. It is these shows to which the comments are geared and not to those isolated events which encourage gardeners to grow bigger vegetables than ever before. The first type of competition involves skill in growing and selection; the second certainly requires skill, but it also necessitates the use of tonnes of fertiliser and manure and appeals more to the glutton than the appreciative gardener.

One thing which applies to any crop that is shown is evenness. If you are asked to show six potatoes or 24 pods of peas, they should be as identical as possible. If you have five large potatoes and one small one, choose in preference six medium-sized ones – uniformity is one of the most important factors in judging.

Specific pests and diseases which may attack your crops are mentioned under each entry. Chapter 10 gives advice on how to cope with them.

GLOBE ARTICHOKE

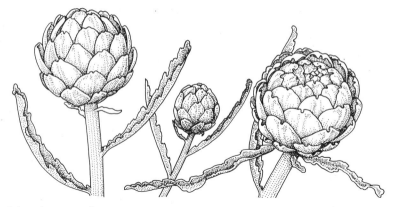

A handsome and statuesque gourmet's vegetable, just as welcome in the flower border as on the vegetable plot. In either situation it needs plenty of room to arch its finely cut grey-green leaves.

VARIETIES

Green Globe and Green Ball are the two varieties most commonly available as seed, but if you take my advice you'll try to obtain some suckers (rooted offshoots) from plants of proven cropping ability. Seed-raised plants can produce scrawny flowerheads hardly worth cooking, but suckers of a variety like Vert de Laon can be relied on.

SITE AND SOIL

A sunny and sheltered site is essential – in very cold districts or in frost pockets globe artichokes will not do well. They are also very greedy, so in the autumn and winter before planting dig over the soil and work in as much well-rotted compost or manure as you can spare – at least two bucket-fuls to each square metre (yard). Just a few days before planting, lightly fork in two handfuls of blood, bone and fishmeal over each square metre (yard).

PLANTING

Plant in spring, spacing your plants 1m (3ft) apart in all direct-ions. Plant with a trowel, firm the soil into place around the roots and then settle the plants in with a good watering.

SEED SOWING

If you cannot obtain young plants from heavy-yielding parents then you'll have to sow seeds outdoors in late March or April. Any ordinary patch of clean, well-worked soil will do as a seedbed provided it is in a warm and sheltered spot (see page 26). Sow the seeds thinly in drills 2.5cm (1in) deep and 30cm (1ft) apart. Thin the seedlings as soon as they are large enough to handle, leaving one every 15cm (6in). Let the plants grow in the seedbed for a year and transplant the health-iest to their permanent spot the following spring.

CULTIVATION

Globe artichokes resent drought so in May topdress the soil around each plant with garden compost or manure. Spread on moist earth the muck will prevent drying out, though in prolonged dry spells a good watering with the hosepipe will be necessary. Remove all flowerheads in the first year so that the plant builds up its strength and all dead stems and foliage in autumn, leaving just a central core of healthy young leaves. Cover these with straw or bracken whenever severe frost threatens and take out any that rot as the winter progresses. Hoe in a handful of sulphate of ammonia around each plant in April to urge it into growth. Feed the plants once a month in the summer with a general liquid fertiliser. When mature plants start to produce flowerheads in the second and successive years, remove the side buds so that only the central one is allowed to develop on each stem. Thin out any overcrowding suckers in spring and use them for propagation. Lift and divide mature plants every four years.

The best way to be sure of a good crop of globe artichokes is to propagate from divisions of a plant that is known to yield plenty of fat flowerheads. You should use a trowel or spade to prise away rooted portions of a mature plant.

HARVESTING

Each mature plant should yield at least 10 fat flowerheads each year. Cut these in summer just as they are plumping up and as the scales at the base are beginning to expand. Don't wait until you can see the flower colour at the top – by then the head will be too far gone to eat. Cut each head with 10cm (4in) of stalk to prevent shrivelling and then remove the rest of the stem from the plant. The flowerheads are relieved of their short stalks immediately before being cooked. Soak the heads in salted water for two hours and then boil them until they are tender. Serve as a starter with lashings of melted butter. The tender leafscale bases and the heart at the bottom of the flowerhead are eaten; the central 'choke' of spiky florets and leathery upper parts of the leaf scales are inedible.

STORAGE

Globe artichokes are not easy to store but if too many of them are ready at once they may be cut with 30-cm (1-ft) long stalks and stood in buckets of damp peat or sand in a cool place. This slows down growth and the buds will stay fresh for several days. Alternatively the gathered heads can be blanched and frozen.

PESTS AND DISEASES

Watch out for slugs and blackfly.

SHOW TIPS

Grow on really deep, rich moisture-retentive soil. Never let the soil dry out. Feed once a week with dilute liquid fertiliser from June to August. Choose the largest heads for showing but make them of even size. They should be plump, firm and fresh – avoid heads that have shrivelled scales or scales which are opening.

IN BRIEF

Site and soil A warm, sunny site and deep, rich soil
Sow Late March/April
Plant April
Harvest July to September from the second year onwards
Effort ***

JERUSALEM ARTICHOKE

A vastly underrated vegetable that makes the best soup I know. It will also add its distinctive earthy flavour to stews and casseroles.

VARIETIES
The ordinary white-skinned variety is like a very knobbly potato which makes it rather difficult to prepare for the pot. Boston Red is similar but has a rosy skin. Fuseau is long, white and usually less knobbly which endears it to impatient cooks. I've grown all three and reckon them all to be tasty and reliable.

SITE AND SOIL
The Jerusalem artichoke will grow almost anywhere so unfortunately it is usually planted in poor soil, but the best crops are produced in a sunny spot on land that is well drained, well cultivated and well manured. Dig the ground in the autumn before planting and work in as much well-rotted compost or manure as you can. The plant is very tall – up to 3.5m (11ft) on my allotment – and makes a good screen for the compost heap or a reasonably sturdy windbreak for more tender plants.

PLANTING
Grow the plants in rows or in clumps. Plant the tubers with a trowel so that they are 15cm (6in) deep and 30cm (1ft) apart. Allow 1.25m (4ft) between separate clumps and rows. Spring is the recommended planting time but I find that the fresher and firmer the tubers are, the healthier the plants will be. To this end I plant shop-bought tubers in November when they are fresh. Mark each row or clump with a short length of cane and label different varieties clearly.

CULTIVATION
Little is needed in the way of coddling. Soak the soil thoroughly only in times of real drought, and draw a little soil around the stems if the tubers become visible.

HARVESTING
When the frost blackens the leaves in autumn, cut down the plants but leave the stem bases to act as markers. Pull soil over the clumps as frost protection. Dig up and harvest the tubers as they are needed and in March lift all those that remain and replant them as for new stock.

Dig up Jerusalem artichokes when you need them at any time between November and March.

PESTS AND DISEASES
Slug damage to the tubers is all you are likely to encounter.

SHOW TIPS

Plant the tubers in a prepared bed of soil that is free of stones and which has been richly dressed with moist peat. Set the tubers 45cm (18in) apart on the square and place them 10cm (4in) deep. Dress the plants with two handfuls of general fertiliser each in April and do not allow the soil to dry out at any time during the summer. Lay a mulch of well-rotted compost or manure after applying the fertiliser dressing. Lift carefully as near to the show date as possible and select large, smooth, shapely tubers with no blemishes. Very knobbly tubers with rough or mottled skin will lose points. Wash the tubers with care to avoid skin damage.

IN BRIEF

Site and soil Unfussy provided drainage is not too poor
Plant November or February/March
Harvest November to March
Effort *

ASPARAGUS

This is a classy vegetable for connoisseurs; it's delicious to eat in its short season but you'll need plenty of patience – new asparagus beds should not be robbed of their bounty until they are in their third season.

VARIETIES

There are several varieties on offer but my first choice would be Regal, closely followed by Connover's Colossal. A new French variety called Minerve has done well in trials at one of the country's research stations, beating other established varieties in the quantity of spears produced.

SITE AND SOIL

Prepare your asparagus bed well in a sunny and sheltered spot. This is not a crop that will be moved around, so it should be pampered right from the start. Dig the soil thoroughly in autumn working in as much well-rotted manure or garden compost as you can spare and removing any perennial weeds. This is important if you are to save yourself hours of backbreaking work later in the season. If your ground is very acid (which means that heathers and rhododendrons grow well on it) then it should be limed before planting. Scatter two handfuls of ground limestone or chalk over each square metre (yard). Repeat this every spring if necessary before the spears emerge.

PLANTING

Sow seeds if you want, but it saves a whole year's toil if you plant one-year-old crowns (which look rather like emaciated dahlia tubers).

Plant the crowns as soon as possible after they arrive to prevent dehydration. If the ground is unfit, then wrap them in damp newspaper until they can be planted with safety. Take out a trench 10cm (4in) deep and 30cm (1ft) wide where the row is to be positioned. Space the crowns 30cm (1ft) apart in the bottom of the trench, spacing out their roots.

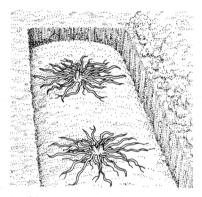

April is asparagus planting time – choose one-year-old crowns and plant them 30cm (1ft) apart in the base of a well-prepared trench.

Return the soil and firm it into place with your feet. If you plan to have more than one row of asparagus, allow at least 60cm (2ft) between the rows to make cultivation easy; or alternatively plant two rows 30cm (1ft) apart and leave 1m (3ft) between each of these double rows to create a 'bed'.

SEED SOWING

If you're really mean and incredibly patient you can raise your asparagus from seeds in April. Soak the seeds overnight in water and then sow them thinly in 2.5-cm (1-in) deep drills on a pre-

pared seedbed in one corner of the plot. Thin the resulting seedlings to leave one every 15cm (6in) and allow them to grow on for a whole year before digging them up in spring and planting them as one-year-old crowns.

CULTIVATION

Make sure that the asparagus does not go short of water at any time. Soak the bed with a hose-pipe whenever drought threatens. Apply liquid feeds at monthly intervals during the first year. In autumn when the foliage turns yellow (but before its fruits ripen and fall), cut it off 2.5cm (1in) above the ground. Spread a 5-cm (2-in) layer of well-rotted compost or manure over the soil when cutting back has been completed.

In the second year a dressing of a general fertiliser can be scattered over the bed in early spring before any shoots emerge. Use blood, bone and fishmeal at the rate of three handfuls to the square metre (yard) and lightly fork it in to the top 5cm (2in) of soil. When the foliage becomes floppy it can be supported with twiggy pea sticks or surrounded by a cane and string enclosure. Keep the bed weed free *at all times*. Cut down and mulch in the autumn as before.

In the third spring continue to apply fertiliser (now an annual operation) and if you want white, blanched stems on your asparagus, draw some soil up from in between the rows to make a mound.

HARVESTING

The asparagus can be cut from late April to late June from the third-season onwards. Use an old kitchen knife or a special asparagus knife with a serrated blade and cut the stems about 8cm (3in) below soil level. Cut all the stems regardless of their thickness – they will all be tasty. Leave the fern to grow from the third week in June – harvest stems later than this and you will severely weaken the plants. A light dressing of fertiliser can be applied after harvesting to give the plants a boost.

STORAGE
You won't have a large enough surplus to store! However, you can freeze some for out-of-season eating if you wish.

PESTS AND DISEASES
Asparagus beetle, slugs and earwigs may be a problem, as can violet root rot.

SHOW TIPS
Never allow the plants to go short of water. Harvest only from mature plants. Feed show plants once a fortnight from April to June with dilute liquid fertiliser. Earth up the stems to blanch the bases. For showing choose the longest, thickest stems which are as straight as possible. They should be a good, fresh colour and the scales should be flat against the stems. There should be no sign of shrivelling.

IN BRIEF

Site and soil A sunny, sheltered site and a rich, weed-free and well-drained soil are essential
Sow April
Plant April
Harvest Late April to late June from the third season onwards
Effort ***

AUBERGINE

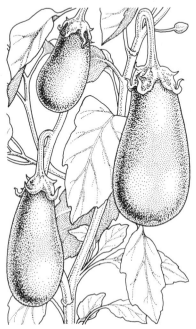

A must for moussaka! The egg-

plant is deservedly popular with gardeners who relish a touch of the exotic. It's always best grown in a greenhouse but it can yield well in good summers in a frame or under tall cloches.

VARIETIES
There are a large number of varieties on offer; I have found both Long Purple and Money-maker to be good – they are both long, dark purple and glossy. Try what takes your fancy, including Easter Egg, a relatively new variety which is white skinned and the same size and shape as a hen's egg.

SITE AND SOIL
Pick the sunniest, most sheltered spot you have for the frame or cloches that will cover aubergines. The soil need not be freshly manured (too much muck will encourage shoot development at the expense of fruits) but it should be in good heart. Two handfuls of blood, bone and fishmeal can be

47

scattered around each plant immediately after planting.

SEED SOWING

Space-sow your seeds 1cm (½in) apart and 0.5cm (¼in) deep in a small pot of seed compost in early to mid-March. Germinate them in a temperature of around 18°C (65°F) – say in the airing cupboard. A polythene bag tied over the pot will keep in humidity. Bring the pot onto a sunny windowsill as soon as the first seedling emerges. Remove the polythene bag after a few days and do not let the compost dry out too much. Try to keep it gently moist – not soggy. Keep the plants warm, and as soon as they are large enough to be handled easily, transfer them individually to 10-cm (4-in) pots of a peat-based potting compost or John Innes No. 2 potting compost. Water them in. Continue to keep the plants warm, watering them when necessary. Pinch out the shoot tip of each plant when it is 12cm (5in) tall to encourage a bushy habit.

PLANTING

In late May or early June (after hardening off and depending on the weather) the plants can be set out under cloches (which should have been put in position two weeks earlier) or in a garden frame. Water each plant before the operation begins. Plant with a trowel, spacing the plants 45cm (18in) apart. Water them in. Keep the cloches or frame closed for a few days (unless the sun shines brightly) to allow them to get over the shock or check to growth.

CULTIVATION

As soon as the flowers open, spray them daily with water to encourage fruit setting. When the fruits start to swell apply a weekly liquid feed of tomato fertiliser. Keep down weeds around the plants and do not let the soil get dry. Allow half-a-dozen fruits to form on each plant – cut off any others and remove the tips of sideshoots to prevent energy being expended on growth. Let too many fruits form and they will all be small. Push a short cane in beside each plant when it is 30cm (1ft) tall. Loosely tie the stem to the cane to prevent it from toppling. From mid-June onwards some kind of shading can be provided. Either whitewash the glass with a proprietary compound, or lay close-weave green plastic netting over the glass in bright weather. Ventilate well at all times, but keep the glass between the plants and the sky!

HARVESTING

Pick the fruits as soon as they are swollen and of a good size but before they turn dull. Shiny fruits are more tasty and tender. Pull up and compost the plants when all the fruits have been picked – watch your hands on those thorns! Aubergines can be sliced, blanched and frozen.

PESTS AND DISEASES

Watch out for aphids, whitefly and red spider mites.

SHOW TIPS

Grow as recommended and make sure the plants do not go short of food or water. Choose large, well

IN BRIEF

Site and soil Sunny, sheltered spot; rich but not over-manured soil
Sow March (indoors) for frame growing; February for greenhouse growing
Plant Late May or early June under cloches or in a frame; April in a greenhouse
Harvest August and September
Effort **

matched fruits which are shapely, glossy, evenly coloured and thick-fleshed. Dull or shrivelled fruits, or those with a blemished skin, will not be thought much of. Black Prince and Large Fruited Slice Rite No. 23 (Unwins) are good show varieties. You will, however always be dependent on a reasonable summer to be sure of success.

BROAD BEAN

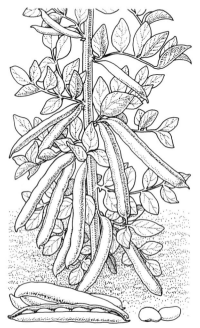

An easy and really rewarding crop for the raw beginner or the expert.

VARIETIES
For autumn and early winter sowings I reckon that The Sutton is hard to beat – it's dwarf and produces heavy crops. Aquadulce is an old standby but it's taller and not so tender. For spring sowings The Sutton still does well, as do the taller Green Longpod and Windsor varieties. Bonny Lad is a promising newcomer which is dwarf and multi-stemmed so it can be planted in single rather than double rows. It should be a good choice for small gardens.

SITE AND SOIL
A spot in full sun and a soil enriched with well-rotted manure or garden compost is what broad beans need to give of their best. Dig and enrich the ground in late summer for autumn sowings and in autumn for spring sowings. Scatter two handfuls of a general fertiliser over each square metre (yard) of ground two weeks before sowing and hoe this in. Acid soil should be limed in winter several weeks after manuring and several weeks before the fertiliser is applied.

SEED SOWING
There's no likelihood of you losing the seeds of broad beans – they're enormous and very easy to handle. Mark out your row with a taut garden line and then go along it with a short stick (or dibber) making 5-cm (2-in) deep holes at 15-cm (6-in) intervals. Drop a seed into each hole and push some soil on top of it. Make another row just 23cm (9in) away from this one and then allow 60cm (2ft) between this double row and the next crop. The autumn and early spring sowings can be covered with cloches if you have any to spare. In severe winters the October to December sowings may be so badly damaged that you have to start again in early spring, but it's often worth the gamble – particularly if cloches can be used.

Alternatively, sow the seeds individually in peat pots in a cold frame in January and plant these out under cloches in March.

CULTIVATION
Hoe regularly between the rows to keep down weeds and ensure that plenty of water is applied in pro-

longed dry spells. Pinch out the shoot tips of the plants when four or five flower clusters have appeared. This concentrates their energy on swelling the pods and it also discourages blackfly attacks. Surround taller varieties with a cane and string enclosure to keep them upright. If the beans are cloched, ventilate thoroughly in mild spells and remove the cloches in April when the weather takes a turn for the better.

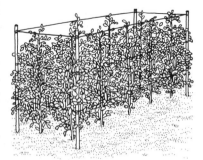

Taller varieties of broad bean can be steadied with a cane and string enclosure to prevent them from nose-diving to the earth in the first heavy breeze.

HARVESTING
Wait until the beans are fat enough to show through the pods and then pick them regularly. Alternatively pick the young pods and cook them whole or sliced as for French beans.

STORAGE
End-of-season surpluses can be frozen or dried.

PESTS AND DISEASES
Blackfly and pea and bean weevil are the only troublesome pests; chocolate spot is the commonest disease.

SHOW TIPS
Enrich the soil as recommended – don't stint on the manure. Keep the soil moist right through the growing season. Choose a longpod variety for showing – Sutton's Exhibition Longpod, Dreadnought and Hylon are recommended. Sow in May and allow only two or three flower trusses to form before pinching out the top of the plant. Apply fortnightly liquid feeds in summer. Select long, fresh, well-filled and bright-coloured pods. The beans inside must be large but they should be tender and not too old. You will lose points for small or crooked pods and for pods which are blemished or unevenly filled.

IN BRIEF

Site and soil Good light and any reasonable soil
Sow October to December; February to June
Successional sowing interval 3 weeks
Harvest June to September
Effort *

FRENCH BEAN

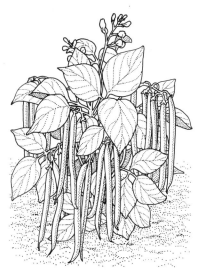

Also known as the kidney bean, this is another easy crop to grow and one which freezes well for winter eating.

VARIETIES

The Prince and Masterpiece are the two oldest and most popular cultivars that seldom disappoint. Newcomers worth trying include Tendergreen which freezes well, Cordon, a fat-podded bean which lasts well on the plant, and Phoenix Claudia which seems to thrive even on light soils. Chevrier Vert is very versatile and can either be cooked in the normal way, or its seeds saved and dried for use in winter soups and stews. Climbing French beans such as Blue Lake are very tender to eat – grow them like runner beans.

SITE AND SOIL

The commonest cause of failure is cold, so only sow when the mild weather arrives and the soil has warmed up. Cloches placed over the soil a couple of weeks before sowing will help to put it in good heart. Dig the ground in autumn, working in as much well-rotted compost or manure as you can spare – the beans like a rich soil and they enjoy the moisture that

such organic matter will retain. Very acid soil should be limed about one month before sowing, and two weeks later a general fertiliser can be applied at the rate of two handfuls to the square metre (yard). Make sure the crop is given a sunny and sheltered site or it will sulk.

SEED SOWING

Sow the seeds in 5-cm (2-in) deep 'V'-shaped drills. Drop one seed every 8cm (3in) along the row and then rake back the soil to cover them. Place cloches over the earliest crops, ventilating them when necessary and remove them completely in late May. Space rows of French beans 45 to 60cm (14 to 18in) apart. When the seedlings emerge remove every other one to leave the plants 15cm (6in) apart.

CULTIVATION

Don't let the plants go short of water. Give the earth a really good soak whenever it is dry a couple of centimetres down. Hoe regularly between the rows and support the plants with twiggy peasticks or canes linked with twine if necessary. Like runner beans the plants will appreciate a mulch of grass clippings in early summer (provided the lawn has not been treated with a weedkiller). Lay the mulch while the soil is moist.

HARVESTING

Pick the beans regularly as soon as they are of a usable size. If they are allowed to mature on the plant, cropping will slow down and the pods will toughen. Late-maturing crops can be protected for a few weeks with tall cloches – put these in place in mid-September. Pull up and compost spent plants.

STORAGE

Any surplus beans can be frozen; the Chevrier Vert type can be pulled from the plants and allowed to dry off before being podded and subsequently stored in jars.

PESTS AND DISEASES

Blackfly and red spider mites are the most likely pests.

SHOW TIPS

Grow as recommended, sowing in May for August shows and paying special attention to watering in dry spells – during the flowering period in particular. Thin the plants to 30cm (1ft) instead of 15cm (6in). The Prince is a variety that still sweeps the board at most shows. The pods should be of even length, straight, fresh and tender (snapping cleanly with no sign of stringiness). No seeds should create lumps in the pod. Pick the beans the day before the show and store them overnight in damp towelling. Take an old length of towel, wet it and then wring it out . Roll one end around a wooden ruler, then insert a bean before giving the fabric another half-roll. Insert more beans, one by one, so that you are making a sort of French bean Swiss roll.

Left tightly rolled all night any beans that are slightly bent will often straighten out while still retaining their freshness.

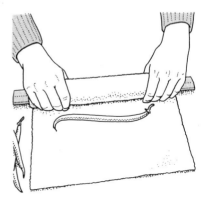

If your show beans are a bit crooked, try rolling them in a length of moist towel the night before the show. A central core consisting of a straight piece of wood should persuade the beans to adopt a more even posture by the time of the show.

IN BRIEF

Site and soil A sunny spot in a fairly rich soil
Sow Under cloches from mid-March to April; in the open from May to July
Successional sowing interval 3 weeks
Harvest July to October
Effort *

RUNNER BEAN

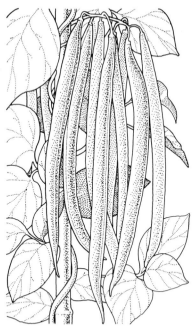

One of the heaviest-yielding vegetable crops and often one of the most decorative. Make sure it doesn't keep the sun off other crops – position the row so that it runs north/south if necessary so that the sun can get around both sides of the row.

VARIETIES

Take your pick from Enorma, Scarlet Emperor, Streamline, Mergoles and Sunset, all of which have grown well for me. The first three produce the largest pods. Kelvedon Marvel is prized by some growers for its ability to crop a couple of weeks earlier than most varieties.

SITE AND SOIL

This is a tall crop so don't position it in a windy spot or where it will cast shade on other vegetables. Use it to screen garden eyesores but make sure that it gets plenty of sun. The soil wants to be as rich as possible – poor earth which dries out will produce only a few very weedy beans. In November of the year before

sowing, take out a trench on the ground to be occupied by the beans. Make it 60cm (2ft) wide and 23cm (9in) deep. Throw into the bottom any organic garden waste – cabbage leaves, carrot tops and anything else that will rot down. Use well-rotted manure or garden compost if you have any to spare, but if you are really short of organic material then fill the trench with torn up newspaper in January immediately before returning the soil. Work two handfuls of a general fertiliser into each square metre (yard) of the soil two weeks before sowing. If the ground is very acid, then apply lime to the surface during the winter and allow the rains to wash it in.

SEED SOWING

Before you commit the seeds to the waiting earth you'll have to rig up a support system for the climbing stems. Runner beans can be grown along the ground but their pods will be small, muddy and misshapen. By far the easiest method of supporting them is the old technique of pushing in two rows of canes 60cm (2ft) apart and tying these together at the top. Use 2.25m (8ft) canes and space

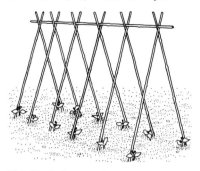

This kind of runner bean support system is one of the best – the beans have plenty of cane to clamber over and picking is easy. Make sure all the ties that hold the canes together are secure. Otherwise you will find that the weight of your crop and gusts of wind might connive to give the structure a drunken lean.

them 35cm (15in) apart in the row. Several more canes are then tied end to end in the little 'V' formed at the cane tips to give stability. Use wire rather than twine for the tying – it is less likely to give out under a heavy crop or a strong breeze. Netting stretched between stout posts makes a fine support but it is extremely tedious to untangle the dead stalks from the mesh at the end of the season. The canes can be freed of vegetation with one deft move of the hand and then stored for use the following year. If you are sowing direct into the ground, wait until a warm spell in May and then plant one seed 5cm (2in) deep at either side of each cane. Pull out one seedling if both seeds grow. Alternatively, sow the seeds individually in peat pots in a cold frame in April and plant one youngster at the foot of each cane in late May.

CULTIVATION

Give the questing shoots a single tie to the cane just to get them on their way – in a matter of two days they will have encircled their support and will be on the upward climb (unless blown off by wind). Hoe between the rows to keep down weeds and give the soil a really good soak if it shows signs of drying out (especially at flowering time). Apply a mulch of grass clippings or garden compost in June while the soil is moist. Pinch out each shoot tip when the top of the cane has been reached. Give the plants one decent liquid feed in August to boost the end-of-season yield.

HARVESTING

Pick the beans regularly as soon as they are of a usable size. Do not wait until they are too large and stringy to be appetising.

STORAGE

Surplus beans can be sliced and frozen as the season progresses. They can also be sliced and stored in salt. Use crushed block salt and place it in alternate 2.5cm (1in) layers with the beans in a large sweet jar. Keep the jar in the dark and soak the beans in plain water for a couple of hours before cooking them. I find them just a bit too salty when they are stored in this way!

PESTS AND DISEASES

Blackfly is the only real problem that attacks with any frequency. If the flowers fail to produce pods the most likely cause is dryness at the roots or poor pollination. Avoid the first by keeping the soil moist, and encourage bees to pollinate the flowers by sowing seeds of borage in April near the site to be occupied by the beans.

SHOW TIPS

Sow under glass in late April – one seed to a 9-cm (3½-in) pot of John Innes No.1 potting compost. Grow on and plant out in the prepared soil (as described above) in early June. Allow the main shoot to extend and pinch out all sideshoots. Remove all but two or three beans from each flower cluster once they start to swell. Make sure the plants do not go short of water at any time. Occasional liquid feeds will be

---

IN BRIEF

Site and soil Enjoys sun, shelter from winds and a very rich soil
Sow April under glass; May and June outdoors
Plant Late May
Successional sowing Unnecessary – one row of beans will crop over a long period
Harvest July to October
Effort **

appreciated. Suitable varieties: Enorma, Crusader, Achievement. Pick the day before the show and wrap overnight as recommended for French beans. Choose the longest, straightest, freshest pods that are not made lumpy by swollen seeds. The pods should be slender rather than fat. Check that a sample pod snaps cleanly with no trace of stringiness.

BEETROOT

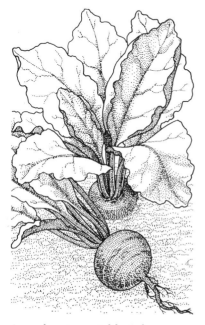

A good root vegetable to keep you supplied with tasty salads and pickles all the year round.

VARIETIES

Use Boltardy for the March and early April sowings as it is resistant to bolting (running to seed instead of forming a fat root). Detroit Little Ball is an oldie that still performs well in summer sowings. It stores well too. If you prefer cylindrical rather than spherical roots choose Cheltenham Greentop. There are also yellow-rooted varieties which add colour variation to boring salads.

SITE AND SOIL

Like most vegetables, beetroot needs sun – the leaves and the roots will be spindly in the shade. But when it comes to soil enrichment it is not so greedy. Give it too much manure and its roots will fork and distort like carrots grown in an over-rich soil. Any reasonable earth that was manured last season or the season before will do nicely for your beetroot, provided that it is not too stony and that it is well forked over before sowing. Two handfuls of a general fertiliser such as blood, bone and fishmeal can be scattered over each square metre (yard) of soil two weeks before sowing. Work this into the surface with a hoe.

SEED SOWING

All sowings made before late March are best covered with cloches until mid-April. Sow the seed capsules 8cm (3in) apart in drills 2.5cm (1in) deep. Space the rows 30cm (1ft) apart for the late spring and summer sowings, but for sowings that are made under cloches it's a good idea to sow a double row 20cm (8in) apart. Each

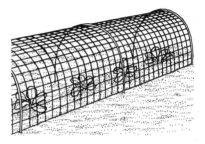

Birds love beetroot plants – protect the young seedlings with tunnels of wire netting if pigeons patrol your allotment.

beetroot capsule contains several seeds and may give rise to a few seedlings. Thin to leave one plant every 8cm(3in) with the spring sowings which will produce smaller roots for early picking. Later sowings can be thinned to leave one plant every 15cm (6in). Seeds of varieties described as 'monogerm' will produce just one seedling from each capsule. This means that less thinning is necessary, but the seeds may have to be sown rather more thickly to avoid gaps in the row.

CULTIVATION
Keep the ground weed free at all times and protect the young plants from birds by erecting small wire mesh tunnels (these can be moved from crop to crop as the need arises). Avoid heavy watering in dry spells for this may cause the roots to swell and split but make sure that the plants do not go short of water in the early stages of growth.

HARVESTING
Pull most roots when they are of a size between a golf ball and a

When you harvest the beetroots, twist off the leaves to prevent the stubs from bleeding - if you cut them off the red sap will ooze out for ages.

tennis ball – that is when they will be at their most tender. Twist off the tops rather than cutting them for this will discourage bleeding. Later sowings intended for winter use can be left in the soil rather longer so that they are a good size by the time they are harvested. As a general rule the first sowings can be harvested in June and July; the May sowings should be lifted in August and the later June and July sowings can be left in the ground until they are needed, provided they are given a covering of straw.

STORAGE
The roots keep well if stored in cardboard boxes in alternate layers with dry peat or sand. They can also be cooked and frozen.

PESTS AND DISEASES
Blackfly may attack the leaves.

SHOW TIPS
Grow in well-cultivated stone-free earth that has not been freshly manured. Sow in May for August shows. Suitable varieties: Detroit New Globe, Boltardy. Try to keep the soil evenly moist at all times. Lift the roots the day before the show and wash them with great care to avoid damaging the skin. Choose evenly spherical roots of a uniform size, about 5cm (2in) in diameter, with small taproots. The flesh should be as dark as possible, but that you can only guess at! Do not cut off the foliage until the last minute (if it has to be cut off), or the root colour may be lost. The skin of the beetroots should be as smooth and clear as possible.

IN BRIEF

Site and soil Plenty of sun and a well-worked soil that is neither too heavy nor too rich in manure
Sow   March to July
Successional sowing interval   4 weeks
Harvest   June onwards
Effort   *

LEAF BEET

Also known as Swiss chard and seakale beet, this is a superb dual-purpose crop which deserves to be more popular: the stalks can be cooked like celery and the leaves like spinach. The plant is so handsome that you may prefer to plant it in the flower border.

VARIETIES
The Swiss Chard or Silver Chard has thick, creamy-white leaf stalks and rumpled glossy green leaves, while Ruby or Rhubarb Chard has rather thinner stalks the colour of cochineal. The white variety is the best type to grow for the pot because it is higher yielding and, I think, more tasty.

SITE AND SOIL
This is a leafy crop which likes a rich soil. Dig over the land in autumn and work in plenty of well-rotted garden compost or manure. Two weeks before sowing scatter two handfuls of blood, bone and fishmeal over each square metre (yard) of ground and lightly fork it in. Greedy as it is, the plant will still survive and crop quite well even on poor soils.

SEED SOWING
Sow the seeds 8cm (3in) apart in drills 2.5cm (1in) deep and 45cm (18in) apart. Thin the seedlings to leave one every 30cm (12in).

CULTIVATION
Routine hoeing and a good soak when the ground is dry are the only operations necessary to grow a good crop.

HARVESTING
Pull off the outer leaves as soon as they are large enough to be usable. Keep harvesting regularly.

STORAGE
The plants can be left in the ground through the winter if they can be given the protection of cloches or straw. In this way they will crop all the year round.

PESTS AND DISEASES
Slugs are the only pests that have ever attacked my Swiss chard.

IN BRIEF

Site and soil   Sunny site, rich and well-drained soil
Sow   May or June
Successional sowing   Unnecessary
Harvest   August onwards
Effort   *

BROCCOLI & CALABRESE

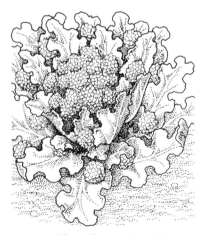

A vegetable with a taste well worth acquiring – broccoli adds a touch of class to any meal and is not very difficult to grow.

VARIETIES

There's a lot of confusion about broccoli and calabrese, but basically the difference is this: purple and white sprouting broccoli matures in late winter and spring; calabrese (the name given to the green-sprouting kind) is not winter hardy and matures in the late summer and early autumn. Early Purple and Late White will give you a succession of heads on your winter crop; Corvet and Express Corona are two reliable calabrese varieties.

SITE AND SOIL

Like all brassicas (members of the cabbage family) broccoli likes a sunny, open site. Dig the soil in the autumn or winter before sowing and work in a reasonable amount of well-rotted garden compost or manure. During the winter dust the ground with lime if it is acid, and in spring trample the ground with your feet to make sure that it is really firm. A week before planting out your young broccoli plants, scatter two handfuls of blood, bone and fish-meal over each square metre (yard) of ground and rake it in.

SEED SOWING

To save space and effort the seeds are sown in a seedbed at one end of the plot (see page 26). Sow the seeds thinly in 1cm (½in) deep drills spaced 23cm (9in) apart and thin the seedlings to leave one every 8cm (3in) when they are 5cm (2in) high.

PLANTING

Plant out the seedlings in the prepared soil as soon as they have reached a height of 8cm (3in). Space them 60cm (2ft) apart within the row, and allow the same distance between rows. Plant with a trowel. The lowest leaves should be just above the soil which should be firmed around the roots with your feet. If that devastating disease clubroot is a problem on your plot, dip the roots of each young plant in a slurry made from a clubroot control containing thiophanate-methyl (e.g. Murphy's Systemic Clubroot Dip). This is the most effective chemical there is for suppressing this dreadful fungus infection. Puddle the plants in once the soil has been firmed (give them 285ml (½ pint) of water each from an open-spouted watering can).

CULTIVATION

As the plants get taller pull some soil around the stems to prevent them from leaning. If the site is very exposed the plants may need staking with short but stout bamboo canes. Hoe regularly between the rows and water thoroughly in dry spells. In July hoe in a little general fertiliser alongside each row of plants.

HARVESTING

Cut the central flowerhead from calabrese as soon as it is 8cm (3in) across – this will encourage the sideshoots to expand and produce some smaller heads. These can be harvested as soon as they are edible and at the latest before severe autumn frosts. Purple and white sprouting broccoli can be picked when ready from late February onwards.

Gather the heads piecemeal from all the plants to keep them producing more shoots. Avoid robbing any plant of all its heads at any one time. Leave broccoli in the ground until the following May; uproot and compost the calabrese plants after stripping them in autumn.

STORAGE
The heads of both crops freeze very well.

PESTS AND DISEASES
As for cabbage (see page 62).

IN BRIEF

Site and soil Sunny site and firm, fairly rich soil that is not too acid
Sow   April and May for broccoli; April to June for calabrese
Plant   June to August
Successional sowing interval   6 weeks
Harvest Calabrese, August to October/November; sprouting broccoli, late February to May
Effort   **

BRUSSELS SPROUT

The worst time to pick Brussels sprouts is when the frost is on them, but that's the best time to eat them for their flavour soars from the buds. They are a marvellous winter standby and the new hybrids seem to produce harder buttons than ever before.

VARIETIES
Peer Gynt is a superb variety which matures as early as September – use it for your first sowing. For the later sowings choose Citadel or the new Widgeon.

SITE AND SOIL
Exactly as for broccoli (see page 58).

SEED SOWING
The earliest sprouts are raised from sowings made in a cold greenhouse in February, but late in that month the seeds can be sown thinly in 1-cm (½-in) deep drills spaced 23cm (9in) apart on a seedbed at one end of the plot provided they can be covered with cloches. Wait until early March if the weather is really foul. Mid-March to April sowings can be made in an unprotected seedbed. Thin the plants to leave them 8cm (3in) apart. Protect from birds if necessary.

PLANTING
Plant out the earliest sowing in

April when the plants are 8cm (3in) high; plant the later sowings in May or June. Plant exactly as for broccoli (including clubroot precautions) and space the plants 60cm (2ft) apart.

CULTIVATION

Hoe regularly between the plants and pull up some soil around the stems about a month after planting. Water thoroughly in dry weather and stake the plants with canes and twine in late summer if the site is at all exposed. In midsummer a sprinkling of general fertiliser can be hoed in alongside each row. In autumn pull off the lower leaves that have turned yellow.

HARVESTING

Snap the sprouts cleanly from the stem as soon as they are large enough to eat. Start at the bottom and work upwards gathering a few buds from each plant. When the plants are exhausted of sprouts, compost the leaves and dispose of the tough stems.

STORAGE

Sprouts stand well in the garden until they are needed but gluts can be frozen.

PESTS AND DISEASES

As for cabbage (see page 62). Soft sprouts (called 'blowers') are formed as a result of the land being too soft or by too much nitrogen being applied after midsummer, or by the land being too heavily manured. The latter is not too common, but if your land is reasonably rich, then plant the sprouts on a patch that was manured for a previous crop rather than on freshly enriched soil.

SHOW TIPS

Grow as recommended. Select the smaller, solid and tightly folded sprouts – not the hefty blowers. They should look as identical as possible and be perfectly fresh. Suitable variety: Roodnerf. The sprout is, however, seldom included in show schedules due to its late maturity.

On windy sites, tall and heavy-cropping Brussels sprout plants should be staked to prevent them from keeling over. Give them a cane apiece and make one tie near the top of the stem.

IN BRIEF

Site and soil   An open, sunny site and rich, firm well-drained soil that is not too acid

Sow   February under cloches or frame; March to April in the open

Plant   April to June

Successional sowing interval   6 weeks

Harvest   September to April

Effort   **

CABBAGE

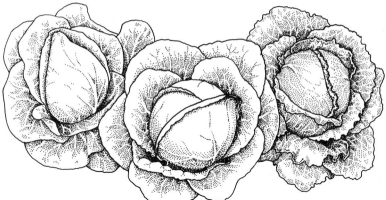

With a bit of careful planning you can make sure of a supply of firm cabbages all the year round.

VARIETIES

There are literally hundreds, but here's what I consider to be the pick of the bunch:

Early summer cabbage – Hispi, Greyhound, Golden Acre; **Summer cabbage** – Derby Day, Wiam, and for the latest crops, Winnigstadt; **Red cabbage** – Ruby Ball, Nigger Head; **Winter cabbage** – Christmas Drumhead, Celtic; **Storing cabbage** – Holland Winter White (see under Storage); **Savoys** – January King, Ormskirk Rearguard; **Spring cabbage** – April, Harbinger, First Early Market No.218.

SITE AND SOIL

Like other brassicas cabbages need a spot in full sun to do well. Choose a piece of ground which has been manured for a previous crop and if it is at all acid, lime it several weeks before planting out. An over-manured patch of soil will produce loose-headed cabbages. Allow cultivated soil to settle for several weeks, and firm it well with your feet before setting out the young plants. Two weeks before planting rake in two handfuls of a general fertiliser to each square metre (yard).

SEED SOWING

Sow in the open in a prepared seedbed, or in a garden frame depending on the timing of the crop. Sow the seeds thinly in 1-cm (½-in) deep drills spaced 23cm (9in) apart. Thin the plants to 8cm (3in) when they are 5cm (2in) high. Protect the seedlings from birds.

PLANTING

As for broccoli (see page 58). Plant spring cabbages 30cm (12in) apart either way; other types 45cm (18in) apart either way. Spring cabbages may be planted at 15-cm (6-in) spacings within the row and as soon as the leaves touch, every other plant can be removed and used as spring greens.

CULTIVATION

Hoe regularly between the rows and remove any leaves that show signs of rotting. Any cabbages maturing through the summer can be given a boost by scattering a little nitrochalk around them (one handful should do three plants). Water thoroughly in the early stages of growth if rainfall is in short supply. Spring cabbages will appreciate a scattering of general fertiliser in April – lightly hoe it into the soil. When spring and summer cabbages have been cut the stumps can be left in the ground and a cross cut in the flat surface with a sharp knife. Young shoots will eventually emerge and can be used as greens or, rather later, as tiny cabbages for they will produce small 'hearts' in the centre.

HARVESTING
Cut the heads when they are usable and place any inedible outer leaves on the compost heap.

STORAGE
Holland Winter White should be cut in November, relieved of its outer leaves and then stored in boxes of dry straw in a shed or garage. The fat, football-like heads can even be placed on a shelf in a cold room and they will remain in good condition until at least February of the following year.

PESTS AND DISEASES
Aphids, flea beetle, cabbage root fly, caterpillars, cabbage whitefly and pigeons are, sadly, common pests of cabbages and other brassicas. Clubroot is the worst disease.

SHOW TIPS
Grow as recommended. The summer-maturing varieties will be those grown for showing. Stonehead, Winnigstadt and Wakker are especially recommended. Choose a fresh, unblemished plant which shows no signs of slug or caterpillar damage (take precautions to keep these pests at bay). The heart should be solid and symmetrical and the outer leaves in perfect condition and of good colour.

IN BRIEF

Site and soil   An open, sunny site and a soil which was manured for a previous crop will grow the best cabbages; the ground should be firm and not too acid

Sow   February and March in a garden frame – early summer cabbage; March to May in the open – summer cabbage, storing cabbage and red cabbage; April and May – winter cabbage and savoys; July to August – spring cabbage

Plant   April and May – early summer cabbage; May to July – summer cabbage, storing cabbage and red cabbage; June and July – winter cabbage and savoys; September to October – spring cabbage

Harvest   June and July – early summer cabbage; August to October – summer cabbage and red cabbage; November – storing cabbage; November to January – winter cabbage; October to March – savoys; April and May – spring cabbage

Effort   **

CAPSICUM

One of my favourites. Although each plant will not yield many fruits, the crop is still worth growing for convenience and for fun. Also known as sweet pepper.

VARIETIES

More capsicum varieties appear every year, but outdoors both Canape and Worldbeater will do well.

SITE AND SOIL

Exactly as for aubergines (see page 47).

SEED SOWING

Exactly as for aubergines.

PLANTING

As for aubergines, but space the plants 30cm (1ft) apart.

CULTIVATION

You've guessed – as for aubergines.

HARVESTING

Pick the fruits as soon as they are of a usable size. They will be glossy and green at first but will turn red if left on the plant. The only difference between green and red peppers is their age. Surplus supplies can be sliced and frozen. Compost spent plants.

PESTS AND DISEASES

Aphids and, occasionally, red spider mites.

SHOW TIPS

Grow as recommended and choose fruits which are fresh, at the peak of perfection and with no sign of shrivelling. The colour (whether green or red) should be bright and even and the skin glossy.

IN BRIEF

Site and soil   Sunny, sheltered spot in good but not freshly manured soil
Sow   March, indoors
Plant   Late May under cloches or in frame
Harvest   August and September
Effort   **

CARROT

More tricky to grow than many folk would have you believe. The secret lies in the preparation of the soil.

VARIETIES

For the earliest crops under cloches or in a frame use Amsterdam Forcing – Amstel, or Early Nantes. Spring sowings of Chantenay Red-Cored – Favourite should yield good summer roots, and for the later sowings, use the old but reliable Autumn King. If your soil is poor and stony try a spherical variety such as Kundulus.

SITE AND SOIL

An open sunny site is essential – only spindly roots will grow in the shade. The best soil for carrots is a light, sandy earth from which stones are absent. Few gardeners are lucky enough to possess this, so to provide the best possible growing conditions, set aside a strip of the vegetable plot for your carrots and really go to town on preparing the soil. Cultivate it thoroughly, forking it through deeply and removing any stones which will cause the roots to fork. Whatever you do, don't add lashings of manure – that too will cause forking – but you can add as much moist, coarse peat as you like to really open up the soil and give the roots a chance to delve down. Two weeks before sowing scatter two handfuls of blood, bone and fishmeal over each square metre (yard) of soil and rake it in.

SEED SOWING

Carrots are such a neat-growing crop that it seems silly to sow them in single rows, leaving 30cm (1ft) between them and the next crop. Instead, take out five or six drills 1cm (½in) deep and only 5cm (2in) apart so that you make a concentrated bed of carrots, saving space and increasing your yield. Sow seeds just half way across the plot at first, and sow the remaining half rows two or three weeks later to give a succession of roots. Sow the seeds very thinly so that you can avoid thinning the seedlings except when some of them are ready to eat. Thin out the youngsters and you will encourage carrot fly. Cover the March-sown carrots with cloches until mid-April, or sow them in a frame and remove the lights at this time.

CULTIVATION

Hoe regularly between the carrot bed and adjacent crops, and hand-pull any weeds that appear between the carrot rows. If the soil shows signs of drying out, water it thoroughly before it loses too much water. Carrots allowed to dry out, which are then soaked to retrieve the situation, will often split.

HARVESTING

Pull the carrots as soon as they are of a usable size. Consign the tops to the compost heap.

STORAGE

Late-maturing carrots can either be covered with straw or bracken and lifted through the winter as they are needed, or they can all be lifted in October, their tops removed and the roots stored in layers in boxes of dry peat or sand. Kept in a shed or garage they should last for several months. Only store roots which are undamaged – bruised and cut roots should be used immediately. Washed and prepared carrots can be frozen.

PESTS AND DISEASES

Carrot fly is the most common pest, but slugs and the carrot willow aphid may also attack.

SHOW TIPS

The best carrots are grown in specially prepared beds. Build a 45-cm (18-in) deep bottomless box on the plot. Make it 45cm (18in) wide and 2m (6ft) or more long, depending on how many carrots you want to grow. Fill the box with sieved garden soil, peat and sand in equal parts, or with old sieved potting compost. Do not incorporate any manure, but give the surface a light dusting of general fertiliser. Prepare the box and compost in January and sow the seeds in April in drills 15cm (6in) apart. Cover the rows with cloches – tent types will fit comfortably on top of the boxes. Gradually harden off the seedlings until the cloches are removed in May. Never allow the soil to dry out – try to keep it evenly moist – sudden drenchings after a dry spell will cause root splitting. Thin gradually to leave the show plants

15cm (6in) apart. Draw soil or peat around the tops of the roots to prevent them from turning green. Guard against carrot fly attack by painting the wooden sides of the structure with timber preservative in early May – the smell will deter the flies. Recommended show varieties: St Valery, Chantenay Red Cored, Nantes Tip Top. Lift the roots carefully the day before the show and wash them to remove soil. Snip off any fine roots. Choose shapely, unforked roots of a good length. Colour should be good and the crown should not be green. Wrap the roots in a damp towel overnight.

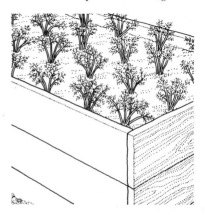

You'll grow the best exhibition carrots on a 45-cm (18-in) deep bed of stone-free compost held in place by wooden boards. Here the roots can penetrate deeply into the hospitable mixture without being diverted by stones. Mind you, don't make the compost too rich or the roots will fork.

IN BRIEF

Site and soil   Open, sunny site and well-cultivated but not freshly manured soil
Sow   March under cloches or frame; April to July in the open
Successional sowing interval   3 weeks
Harvest   June to October
Effort   *

CAULIFLOWER

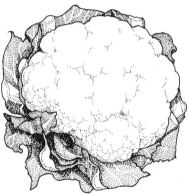

These are the gluttons of the vegetable plot and will only give you a good return if you dine them well.

VARIETIES
This is another confusing vegetable because the winter-maturing varieties are sometimes referred to as 'winter broccoli'. Here I shall stick to calling them winter cauliflower because on my plate that's what they are! **Summer-heading varieties**: Alpha, Dominant, Snowball, All The Year Round; **autumn-heading varieties**: Flora Blanca (August and September), Barrier Reef (October and November), Autumn Giant (November and December); **winter-heading varieties**: Snow's Winter White (January and February), Early Feltham (March), Walcheren Winter (April and May), Asmer Juno (May and June).

SITE AND SOIL
Pick a sunny and sheltered site for your cauliflowers, avoiding frost-pockets for the winter varieties. The soil should be well dug in autumn and as much well-rotted garden compost or manure dug in as you can lay your spade on. On dry ground cauliflowers will never amount to much, so make sure that the earth will hold on to plenty of moisture in summer (this does not mean that it should be waterlogged at other times of year!). Allow the ground to settle

thoroughly before planting, and a couple of weeks before setting out the young plants, trample the soil and work in two handfuls of a general fertiliser to each square metre (yard).

SEED SOWING
There are three ways of raising the summer-heading cauliflowers. They can be sown in 1-cm (½-in) deep drills 23cm (9in) apart in an outdoor seedbed in late September and transplanted 10cm (4in) apart under cloches or into a frame the following month. In the following March or April they are transplanted at their final spacing. Alternatively, sow the seeds in trays of compost in a greenhouse heated to a temperature of 13°C (55°F) in February. Prick out the young plants individually into peat pots and then harden them off prior to planting out in April. If you have no protection to offer the plants, sow outdoors in a prepared seedbed in March and April. Autumn and winter heading types are sown outdoors in April and May.

PLANTING
When the plants are 8 to 10cm (3 to 4in) high they can be transplanted at their final spacings. Water the seedbed thoroughly the day before lifting the young plants so that they receive as little check as possible. Plant them with a trowel, firming the soil around their roots with your feet and then puddling them in with a watering can or slow-running hosepipe. Plant the summer-heading varieties 45cm (18in) apart and allow 60cm (2ft) between rows. The autumn and winter heading types will make larger plants so allow 60cm (2ft) between them and 75cm (2½ft) between the rows.

CULTIVATION
Hoe regularly between the rows and give the soil a thorough soak if it looks like becoming too dry. Scatter a little sulphate of ammonia around the plants during

the summer if growth is at a standstill – one handful should do three plants. As the curds (white centres) begin to swell, break a couple of leaves inwards over them so that they are kept fresh and white.

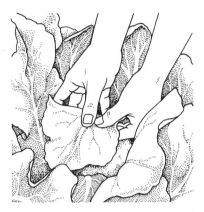

When the curds on your cauliflowers start to come to maturity, protect them by bending over one or two of the inner leaves. It will keep the centre crisp, white and unblemished.

HARVESTING
Cut the curds as soon as they are usable but before the flower sections separate. Place the unwanted leaves on the compost heap and dispose of the stumps.

STORAGE
Cauliflower freezes very well, but mature heads can also be stored in a shed or garage in boxes of straw where they will keep in good condition for a month or more. Winter types should withstand most weather, but in very severe conditions they will benefit from being cloched.

PESTS AND DISEASES
See cabbage (page 62). Cauliflowers that produce loose curds or which run to flower prematurely have not been grown in firm ground. A lack of curds usually indicates either that the plants have received a check at some stage in their growth (probably as a result of water shortage) or that the ground is not rich enough in organic matter.

SHOW TIPS
March sowings will yield show material. Grow as recommended taking particular care to ensure that the plants never go short of water. Dok and All The Year Round are good showing varieties. Choose a plant with a large, symmetrical, tight curd which is not showing any gaps. It should be as white and fresh-looking as possible with no blemishes. Remove the leaves as close to showing time as possible, leaving intact the small ones that directly embrace the curd.

IN BRIEF

Site and soil A sunny site and a very rich, firm, moisture-retentive soil are essential

Sow Late September in the open for winter cloching – summer heading; February in a heated frame or greenhouse – summer heading; March and April in an open seedbed – summer heading; late April to mid-May in an open seedbed – autumn and winter heading

Plant March to May – summer heading; June and July – autumn and winter heading

Harvest June and July – summer heading; August to May – autumn and winter heading

Effort **

CELERIAC

Don't bother with 'turnip-rooted celery' unless you can really give it a rich diet to produce fat roots worth harvesting. Grown well it is a useful vegetable for soups and stews.

VARIETIES
Most seedsmen sell only one variety so you'll have to shop around to find the one you want. There's not much to choose between Alabaster, Marble Ball, Globus and Tellus. The newcomer Jose looks promising and is supposedly quicker to mature than other varieties.

SITE AND SOIL
Choose a sunny and sheltered spot for your celeriac and make the ground really rich and moisture retentive. Work in plenty of well-rotted compost or manure in the autumn before planting. It's even worth taking out a trench (as if you were growing runner beans) and filling it with rotted organic matter before returning the soil. Starve your celeriac and it will not

be worth growing. Two weeks before planting, scatter two handfuls of blood, bone and fishmeal over each square metre (yard) of ground and rake it into the surface.

SEED SOWING
The seeds need warmth to germinate. Sow in a heated frame or greenhouse if you can, and prick out the seedlings into trays of a peat-based potting compost as soon as they are large enough to handle. Harden them off prior to planting out. Alternatively, sow the seeds under cloches in early April, thin out the seedlings and then transplant the remaining ones to their permanent site when they are 8 or 10cm (3 or 4in) high.

PLANTING
Soak the young plants immediately before they are planted in their prepared soil. Set them 30cm (1ft) apart in rows 45cm (1½ft) apart. Plant them firmly and not too deeply – the stem bases should be at ground level.

CULTIVATION
Never let the soil around the plants dry out. If you can spare the time, give them a liquid feed once a week during the summer. Remove any yellowing leaves, and gradually remove some of the lower ones as the stem bases start to swell. Pull off any sideshoots that appear. Hoe regularly between the rows to keep down weeds.

HARVESTING
From September onwards the roots can be pulled up and used as required.

STORAGE
Lift all remaining plants in October, trim off the leaves and store the roots in boxes of dry sand or peat kept in a cool place. Alternatively spread straw or bracken over the plants to protect them from frost. Continue harvesting until the following spring when all remaining roots can be lifted to make way for new crops.

PESTS AND DISEASES
As for celery, though few serious problems will be encountered.

SHOW TIPS
Grow as recommended. Choose deeply globular roots for showing. They should be as smooth as possible and trimmed of any hairy roots. Wash the root carefully and cut back the leaves. The new variety Jose should be worth a try on the showbench.

IN BRIEF

Site and soil A sunny spot in a very rich soil that is unlikely to dry out
Sow March in a warm frame or greenhouse; early April under cloches
Plant Late May or early June
Successional sowing Unnecessary
Harvest September to October
Effort ***

CELERY

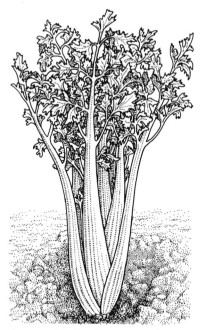

A vegetable for the patient, keen gardener who enjoys a challenge as much as he does crispy salads!

VARIETIES
Golden Self-blanching is the first to mature, followed by the popular American Green which lasts until the frosts. The traditional varieties offered vary in their colour and little else – try Giant White, Giant Pink or Giant Red.

SITE AND SOIL
All types of celery like a sunny and sheltered spot in a part of the plot that is not a frost pocket. The soil should be enriched as much as possible and not liable to summer drying. For the self-blanching types of celery work in as much well-rotted garden compost or manure as you can spare when you are autumn or winter digging the site. About a week before setting out the young plants, scatter three handfuls of a general fertiliser over each square metre (yard) of soil and rake it in. Traditional celery needs to be earthed up with soil if it is to turn white and crisp, so a different (and more energetic) approach is needed. Dig a trench 38cm (15in) wide and 30cm (1ft) deep where the row of celery is to be positioned. Spread a thick layer of compost or manure in the bottom and then return the soil to within 10cm (4in) of the top – leaving the surplus soil in even ridges down either side of the trench. The

Traditional celery is planted in trenches. The soil at the sides will eventually be returned around the plants as they grow, making their leaf stalks white and crisp.

plants will be set out in the hollow and the soil gradually replaced (see Cultivation).

SEED SOWING
Sow the seeds in pots or trays in a greenhouse or frame heated to a temperature of 16°C (60°F). Prick out the seedlings as soon as they are large enough to handle. Use a peat-based potting compost for this operation and thereafter do not let the youngsters get too cold or they are likely to run to seed before fattening up their leaf stalks. Gradually harden off the young plants until late May or early June when they can be planted out.

PLANTING
Traditional celery should be planted in a single row down the centre of the trench. Space the plants 15cm (6in) apart. Self-blanching celery is planted in 'blocks' on level ground so that the light is excluded from most plants by virtue of the fact that they are overcrowded. Space the plants 23cm (9in) apart either way. Plant both kinds of celery with a trowel and water all the plants in quite thoroughly.

CULTIVATION
Traditional celery Water thoroughly whenever the soil starts to look dry. Remove any sideshoots the plants produce and also any weed growth. When the plants are 30cm (1ft) high, loosely fasten a cylinder of thin card or newspaper around

each plant and earth up with 8cm (3in) of soil. A light dusting of a general fertiliser can be scattered onto the soil around the plants before this first earthing up. Make sure the soil is moist when you earth up, and do the job twice more at roughly three-week intervals. Try to prevent soil from falling in among the leaves. When the final earthing up is carried out the leaves should be protruding above the soil but all the stalks should be covered. A mound will have replaced the trench.

A cardboard collar placed around each plant before earthing up means that less grit should find its way on to your plate.

Self-blanching and green celery
This crop needs no soil adjustment. It is sufficient instead to spread bracken or straw around the outer plants in early July to exclude light from their stalks. Again a sprinkling of fertiliser among the plants in summer will give them a boost.

HARVESTING
Pull up self-blanching and green plants as soon as they are large enough to be usable. Try to start at the outside of the block and work inwards. Harvest all the crop before frosts become frequent. Traditional 'trenched' celery will

withstand quite a lot of frost if its foliage is covered with dry straw or bracken. Pull away the soil and remove a plant when you need it.

STORAGE

Celery can be frozen provided that it will be cooked before eating (the flesh deteriorates too much for it to be eaten raw).

PESTS AND DISEASES

Soft rot, celery fly and celery leaf spot are the only likely problems.

SHOW TIPS

Grow as recommended, taking especial care with the watering – plenty of it! Instead of earthing the plants up, wrap the leaf stalks in thick paper or thin card – making a cylinder around them.

Gradually extend this paper blanching up the stalks as they extend. (The traditional earthing up acts as frost protection, but as this celery is harvested in August it is not necessary and only dirties the stalks.) Apply weekly liquid feeds in summer. It is the traditional celery that wins the prizes. Choose large plants for showing. They should be tightly . packed, well-blanched, clean and unblemished. No flower heads should be visible, nor should any pests. Remove the fibrous roots from the base and tie the stems together just below the leaves. The leaf stalks should be thick and crisp.

IN BRIEF

Site and soil A sunny, sheltered site and a rich, well-manured soil are essential requirements

Sow Late March or April in a warm frame or greenhouse

Plant Late May and early June

Successional sowing Unnecessary

Harvest Late July until October – self-blanching and green types; October to February – traditional types

Effort ** (self-blanching) **** (traditional)

CHICORY

Chicory is not to everybody's taste but it is quite costly in the shops and worth growing if you value its crispy winter leaves.

VARIETIES
For forcing use Witloof or Normato. For fresh winter chicory try Winter Fare, Sugar Loaf or the new Crystal Head which usually lasts until March in the open garden.

SITE AND SOIL
Any ordinary, well-cultivated soil that was manured for a previous crop will grow some good chicory. This is a large-leaved crop which needs good light.

SEED SOWING
Sow the seeds thinly in 1-cm (½-in) deep drills spaced 30cm (1ft) from any adjacent crop. As soon as the seedlings are 5cm (2in) high thin them to a spacing of 23cm (9in).

CULTIVATION
Hoe regularly alongside the row to keep down weeds. Water the ground thoroughly in dry spells to keep the plants growing, and apply a liquid feed in summer if growth is slow.

HARVESTING
Forcing types In November, cut off all the foliage 2.5cm (1in) above ground level (not too close or you'll damage the growing point). Lift the parsnip-like roots, discarding any which are less than finger-thick. Trim off the bottom of each selected root so that just the upper 15cm (6in) remains and store these prepared portions horizontally in boxes of moist sand in a cold but frostproof shed or garage. They can be kept there for several months. When chicons are needed pot up three roots to a 23-cm (9-in) pot of moist peat or old potting compost so that the leaf bases are showing above the compost. Stand the pot in a *thick* black polythene bag and knot the top so that it is light proof. Stand the covered pot in a dark cupboard where the temperature

Pot up three chicory roots to a 23-cm (9-in) pot of compost and stand them in a warm, dark place. Keep all light out and the compost gently moist, and in a few weeks you'll have three fat chicons to perk up winter salads.

hovers between 13 and 21°C(55 and 70°F) and check it every few days. Water the compost if it feels dry. The fat chicons will be ready to cut in two to four weeks time. They should be white and crisp; if they are yellow or pale green and taste excessively bitter, then your blacking out has not been effective. Discard the roots after forcing. Plants can also be left in the ground and forced, though they will not appear until February or March the following year. After cutting down in the autumn, make a 15-cm (6-in) mound of soil over the row and pat it firm with the back of a spade. A portion of the row can be covered with cloches to hasten development. Uncover the chicons and cut them immediately before they are to be used.

Unforced chicory The later sown chicory is rather like a cos lettuce to look at and its tangy flavour perks up winter salads. It stands well in the open garden but its life can be reliably prolonged and its condition improved if it is covered in November with cloches.

PESTS AND DISEASES
Only slugs will be a problem, and aphids may occasionally infest the leaves.

IN BRIEF

Site and soil Sunny site; ordinary well-drained soil
Sow May or June for forcing; Mid-June to mid-July non-forcing
Successional sowing Unnecessary
Harvest November for winter forcing; October to December for non-forcing types
Effort **

CORN SALAD

A pleasant change to lettuce, corn salad or lamb's lettuce is easy to grow and needs little in the way of attention and space.

VARIETIES
The type sold by most seedsmen is described as 'Large Leaved'.

SITE AND SOIL
Provided it has plenty of sun, corn salad is unfussy about soil but certainly makes a better contribution to your salads if the earth is richer rather than poorer. Sow it on ground that has been manured for a previous crop. If it is sown in late summer for its useful winter leaves, then soil which has been cropped through the summer need only be lightly cultivated prior to sowing.

SEED SOWING
Sow the seeds thinly in 1-cm (½-in) deep drills spaced 23cm (9in) apart. Thin the seedlings to 10cm (4in) when they are a couple of centimetres high.

CULTIVATION
Routine hoeing and watering in summer are all that is necessary.

HARVESTING
Pull the outer leaves as soon as the plants are of a size to withstand this defoliation. Dry bracken or straw will give the plants welcome protection through the winter, but cloches are even more efficient.

PESTS AND DISEASES
None to speak of.

IN BRIEF

Site and soil Sunny spot, ordinary soil
Sow August or September for winter and spring harvesting; March or April for summer harvesting
Successional sowing Unnecessary
Harvest November to March – August/September sowing; June onwards – March/April sowing
Effort *

CUCUMBER

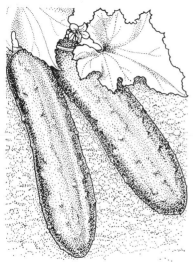

Those long cucumbers you buy in the shops need a heated greenhouse to bring them to perfection, but there are shorter ridge and Japanese cucumbers that will do well with cloche or frame cover.

VARIETIES
The most reliable varieties are the Japanese kinds of which Kyoto and Burpless Tasty Green are readily available. Burpee Hybrid is also highly praised by many gardeners.

SITE AND SOIL
Choose a sunny, sheltered spot and enrich the soil well. The best way to do this is to dig a hole 30cm (1ft) square and as much deep and three-quarters fill it with well-rotted manure or compost before replacing a 15-cm (6-in) layer of soil. Do this at every planting site (for spacing see below). If planting under cloches, put these in place two weeks before planting.

SEED SOWING
Sow the seeds individually 2.5cm (1in) deep in 8-cm (3-in) diameter peat pots of a peat-based compost such as Levington, Kerimure or Arthur Bowers. Sow more seeds than you need to allow for a few failures. Water them in and place the pots in a seed tray. Envelop this in a polythene bag and then put the lot in the airing cupboard where a temperature of about 18 or 21°C (65 or 70°F) is maintained. As soon as the first seedling shows, remove the tray from the cupboard and stand it on a bright windowsill. Remove the plastic bag after a few days. Keep the plants well watered. Space them out to allow development, and harden them off prior to planting out. Seeds can also be sown outdoors under cloches where they are to grow in May or June. Sow two seeds at each station and thin to leave the healthiest plant.

PLANTING
Water the plants well before planting. Plant with a trowel on the prepared mound of soil, spacing the plants 75cm (2½ft) apart. Give them cloche or frame

cover immediately. Although the Japanese cucumbers can be trained up tripods of canes in warm districts, it is a good idea to grow them under frames and cloches in all other areas. A handy way of supporting plants grown under cover is to lay a narrow strip of trelliswork over bricks placed between the plants. This will keep the fruits off the ground, so preventing both slug and fungus attacks.

Prevent the fruits of outdoor cucumbers from becoming soiled and slug-eaten by supporting them on a length of trelliswork balanced on bricks.

CULTIVATION
Never let the soil around the plants dry out. Remove all weed growth. Pinch the shoot tip after half a dozen leaves have formed and pinch out sideshoot tips to keep the plants within bounds. Mulch the soil around each plant with well-rotted manure in July to keep in moisture. Feed once a week from July onwards using a liquid tomato fertiliser. The plants will enjoy a daily misting with water if you can spare the time. Ventilate well on warm days and shade the glass during bright sunshine from planting onwards as the leaves are very easily scorched. Unlike greenhouse-grown cucumbers, the outdoor types do not need to have their male flowers removed.

HARVESTING
Cut and use the cucumbers as soon as they are of a usable size, but remember that they are likely to be only 15 to 23cm (6 to 9in) long rather than 45cm (1½ft).

PESTS AND DISEASES
Whitefly, red spider mite, slugs and mosaic virus are the commonest problems. Mildew may occur if the plants are badly ventilated.

SHOW TIPS
Grow as recommended and remember that for showing you will need a pair of cucumbers which should be as identical as possible. They should be fresh, tender, straight and of equal thickness and they should still have faded flowers attached to their ends. Avoid choosing fruits which have not reached maturity, but conversely don't exhibit old ones. If the cucumbers are of different sizes, harvest one in advance of the other so that the remaining fruit can catch up.

IN BRIEF

Site and soil Rich, moisture-retentive soil in a sunny spot
Sow April, indoors
Plant Late May or early June under cloches or in a frame
Harvest Mid-July to September
Effort ***

ENDIVE

An acquired taste, but one well worth acquiring. Endive makes a much more flavoursome substitute for lettuce and is unsurpassable in wholemeal bread sandwiches. Some varieties look like frizzy-leaved lettuces; others have broader leaves.

VARIETIES
Green Curled or Moss Curled are good frizzy kinds to sow for summer and autumn use; Batavian Broad-Leaved is the variety which will stand well into winter for those cold-weather salads.

SITE AND SOIL
Endive is valued as a winter vege-table in many households, but although summer crops are happy in the open, the winter crop needs protection under glass. The soil should be well cultivated and well manured in winter, and the spot should be as sunny as possible – especially for late-maturing crops. Clay soil will sometimes be toler-ated but it is not enjoyed.

SEED SOWING
Sow the seeds outdoors where they are to grow in drills 1cm (½in) deep and 30cm (1ft) apart. Sow the seeds thinly and thin the resulting seedlings first to 8cm (3in) and later to 23cm (9in). Late sowings should be made under cloches and the plants thinned to 30cm (1ft) to allow them more room to grow.

CULTIVATION
Hoe regularly between the rows and water well in dry weather. Endive likes to be grown without a check. When the plants reach a diameter of 23cm (9in) they can be blanched in succession to produce an even supply of hearts. Un-blanched endive is very bitter, so the exclusion of light is necessary to produce palatable crops. Cover the plant to be blanched with a 20- or 23-cm (8- or 9-in) flowerpot, after first blocking up the holes in the base so that no light is admitted. Make sure the plant has dry leaves before you blanch or fungal rot may set in. Keep the pot in place for three weeks and use

Blanch endives by covering them individually with a flowerpot whose holes have been blocked to exclude light.

IN BRIEF

Site and soil Sunny spot; well-manured soil
Sow Late March to August – frizzy; July to early September – broad leaved
Successional sowing interval 4 weeks
Harvest August to March (winter supplies protected with cloches)
Effort ***

the plant when it is yellowish white all over. Cover all endives with cloches in early September, or sow them in a frame and put the lights in position at this time.

HARVESTING
From August through until March, blanching at intervals to produce a succession.

PESTS AND DISEASES
Slugs and aphids may take a nibble.

SHOW TIPS
Grow as recommended and time your blanching for the show. Choose a plant which is perfectly formed and of a good shape and make sure it is evenly blanched. It should be tender and free from pest attack. Don't exhibit a wilting, poorly grown plant.

KALE OR BORECOLE

Curly kale is such a good-looking crop that it's hard to resist growing it. It's as hardy as old boots in winter and a reliable source of spring greens.

VARIETIES
Pentland Brig is very reliable and vigorous but it's not so frilly as Dwarf Green Curled (good for small plots) or Tall Green Curled (where there is more space). Frosty is a dwarf curled variety that grows to only 30cm (1ft) and which has proved to last exceptionally well.

SITE AND SOIL
Choose an open spot and a patch of soil which was manured for a previous crop. Dig the ground well in the autumn before sowing and apply lime if it is acid. Two weeks before planting out dust the soil with two handfuls of a general

fertiliser over each square metre (yard) and hoe it in. Make the ground firm.

SEED SOWING
Sow the seeds thinly in 1-cm (½-in) deep drills spaced 23cm (9in) apart in a prepared seedbed at one end of the plot (for preparation see page 26). Thin the seedlings as soon as they are 2.5cm (1in) high, leaving them 8cm (3in) apart. Thin later to leave them 15cm (6in) apart.

PLANTING
Plant out the youngsters when they are 10 to 12cm (4 to 5in) high, spacing them 35cm (15in) apart and allowing 45cm (18in) between rows. Water the seedbed the day before shifting them, and give the plants a good soaking when they have been planted in their prepared soil. Plant with a trowel and firm the roots into place with your feet.

CULTIVATION
Hoe regularly between the plants and the rows, and soak the soil thoroughly in times of drought. Pick off faded lower leaves as soon as they are seen. In March or April scatter some general fertiliser around the plants and hoe it in – one handful will do two plants.

HARVESTING
Pentland Brig yields both leaves and flowering shoots which make tasty meals. Others produce plenty of curly leaves come the

spring. Harvest them all on a cut and come again system. Storage is unnecessary as the plants stand well on the plot.

PESTS AND DISEASES
As for cabbage (see page 62), though less affected by clubroot.

IN BRIEF

Site and soil An open site and any ordinary well-nourished soil
Sow April and May
Plant June to August
Successional sowing Unnecessary
Harvest November to May
Effort **

KOHLRABI

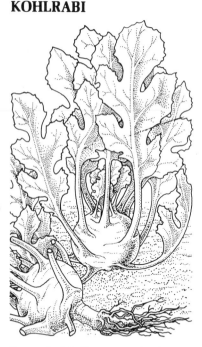

It's undoubtedly an acquired taste but I find kohlrabi a refreshing change from other root vegetables. The secret of producing the tastiest roots is to grow them quickly and harvest them small.

VARIETIES
White Vienna and Purple Vienna are the varieties offered by nearly every seedsman. Both are tasty and tender with a flavour that is a combination of cabbages and turnips.

SITE AND SOIL
Pick a sunny spot for your kohl-rabi and dig the soil thoroughly in the autumn or winter prior to sowing. Land manured for a previous crop is best so that this vegetable will grow speedily but not too leafily. Apply lime after digging if the soil is acid, and scatter three handfuls of blood, bone and fishmeal over each square metre (yard) of soil two weeks before sowing the crop. Rake this nourishment in.

SEED SOWING
Sow the seeds thinly in drills 1cm (½in) deep and 30cm (1ft) apart. Thin the seedlings to leave them 15cm (6in) apart as soon as they are 5cm (2in) high.

CULTIVATION
Give the ground a thorough soaking whenever it shows signs of being dry a few centimetres down. Hoe regularly between the rows and hand weed among the plants. If growth is slow, apply a liquid feed when the plants are six weeks old.

HARVESTING
Pull the roots (or, more accurately, the swollen stems) just before they reach tennis ball size. Let them grow any fatter and they will become woody. The leaves can be

cooked like spinach and the roots are boiled without being peeled. They're delicious with white sauce.

STORAGE

It's not worth the bother. The stems deteriorate rapidly in store, so are best left in the ground and pulled as required.

PESTS AND DISEASES

As for cabbages (see page 62), but as this is a quick-growing crop only quick-acting pests and diseases usually strike. Pigeons are a menace and greenfly can be a minor nuisance.

IN BRIEF

Site and soil Light, rich soil produces the best crop; plenty of light is needed

Sow Late March to June – white variety; June to August – purple variety

Successional sowing interval 3 weeks

Harvest Late June to December

Effort *

LAND CRESS

If you love watercress but lack a stream, try growing land cress. Washed under the tap and sand-wiched between two slices of wholemeal bread it tastes delicious!

VARIETIES

The type described as American or Land Cress is the one to buy.

SITE AND SOIL

If you've a shady patch on your plot try the cress there. It likes a rich piece of earth so dig the soil and work in compost or manure in the months before sowing.

SEED SOWING

Sow the seed thinly in 1-cm (½-in) deep drills spaced 23cm (9in) apart and thin the seedlings to 15cm (6in). Sow small batches for a succession and make sure the soil is moist at sowing time.

CULTIVATION

Routine hoeing and a soak when the soil is dry is all this obliging little vegetable needs.

HARVESTING

Pull the leaves and sprigs as they are required when the plants are a couple of months old.

IN BRIEF

Site and soil Lightly shaded spot; very rich, moisture-retentive soil

Sow March to September

Successional sowing interval 3 weeks

Harvest May to February

Effort *

STORAGE

Not necessary for early-sown crops, but later sowings will benefit from a straw or cloche covering from November onwards.

Pull up and compost the plants in late spring.

PESTS AND DISEASES

Aphids are likely to be the only real problem.

LEEK

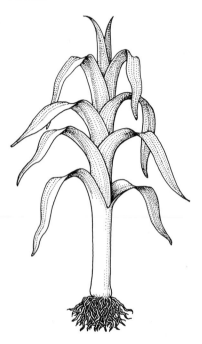

Indispensable on my vegetable plot, the leek is one of the tastiest and most reliable of all crops.

VARIETIES

Walton Mammoth is one of the earliest varieties to mature, but for later crops the old reliable Musselburgh or the new Catalina are the best choices.

SITE AND SOIL

On a sunny part of the plot, dig the ground thoroughly in the autumn or winter before planting and work in as much organic matter as you can spare. The leeks will still grow on ordinary soil but their stems will be relatively thin and your yields lower than they

should be. Scatter three handfuls of a general fertiliser over each square metre (yard) of ground a week before planting and lightly hoe it in.

SEED SOWING

Although they can be raised earlier in a greenhouse or frame, I like to sow my leeks outdoors in March or early April. It's less bother and although the plants mature a few weeks later the wait makes them that much more enjoyable. Sow the seeds thinly in 1-cm (½-in) deep drills spaced 23cm (9in) apart on a seedbed at one end of the plot (for preparation see page 26). Water the seedlings thoroughly in dry spells and leave them in the seedbed until they are 20 to 25cm (8 to 10in) high.

PLANTING

When the seedlings are large enough to be transplanted, soak

Planting young leeks is a satisfying job. Shorten the leaves by one third and the roots by one half, then drop the plants into prepared dibber holes 15cm (6in) deep. Now water them in.

the seedbed a few hours before-hand. When you are ready to plant lift the seedlings with a fork. Choose the most vigorous ones first and shorten their leaves by about one-third and their roots by one half. Mark the position of the row with a taut garden line and make 15-cm (6-in) deep holes at 10-cm (4-in) intervals with a piece of broom handle or a large dibber. Drop one young plant into each hole and then fill the hole with water. That's all there is to it – the soil will eventually fall back by itself and a good portion of the stem should be blanched. The less vigorous seedlings can be planted if there is a shortage of fatter ones, but otherwise discard them. Allow 30cm (1ft) between the planted rows.

CULTIVATION
Turn a sprinkler on the soil in dry weather to give it a good soak. Hoe regularly between the rows. If you can spare the time give the plants two or three liquid feeds during the summer – the more generous you are the fatter will be the stems (feed them once a week if you like!).

HARVESTING
Lift the leeks as soon as they are of a usable size and as you need them. They will stand perfectly well in the garden until the follow-ing spring so no storage is necessary. When the soil they occupy is needed for other crops, lift them and 'heel them in' on one corner of the plot: take out a 'V'-shaped trench 20cm (8in) deep, lay the leeks in at an angle of 45° and replace the soil.

PESTS AND DISEASES
Leek rust is really the only problem likely to be encountered.
SHOW TIPS
To produce leeks for August shows you'll have to sow under glass in January. Plant out in May in very rich, moisture-retentive soil, having hardened the plants off thoroughly. Make sure the plants do not go short of water, and when they are 45cm (18in) high, either surround their stems with thin card to blanch them, or slide over them 30-cm (1-ft) lengths of plastic drainpipe,

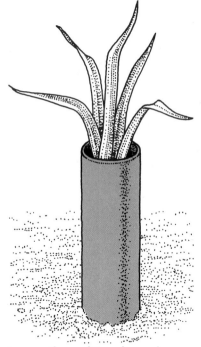

Improve the condition of your show leeks by blanching them inside a length of narrow plastic drainpipe.

IN BRIEF

Site and soil Open and sunny site; soil as rich as possible
Sow March and April in the open
Plant June and July
Successional sowing Unnecessary
Harvest November to May
Effort **

pushing the base of the pipe into the soil. Apply dilute liquid feeds fortnightly in summer. Suitable varieties include Robinson's Mammoth Blanch Leeks, Lyon – Prizetaker and Snowstar. Choose plants that are thick and straight, with long, well-blanched bases.

There should not be any sign of bulbousness at the base – the stem should be of an even thickness. The skin should be flawless. The leeks are usually tied in bundles, but a little of the foliage should be removed.

LETTUCE

With a bit of planning you can enjoy lettuces for nine months of the year with no more than a few cloches to see your plants through the hard times. Growing winter lettuces is certainly a chancy business, but good results make the heartache worthwhile.

VARIETIES

There are many lettuce varieties of different shapes and seasons of maturity so here's my simplified list of some of the best whose sowing times are given above. (C = Cos – superb, long, crispy leaves; B = butterhead – soft-leaved, round, cabbage-headed types; Cr = crisphead – rounded in shape but with crispy-crunchy leaves.) Winter Density (C) dark green, rich flavour; Unrivalled (B) soft and tender; Tom Thumb (B) small, sweet and crisp; Little Gem (C) crisp, sweet and compact; Barcarolle (C) rich green, crisp and sweet; Webb's Wonderful (Cr) large, firm and crisp; Salad Bowl – frilly, non-hearting, very tasty and ornamental; Avondefiance (B) round and tender, mildew-resistant; Continuity (B) tasty and colourful – leaves are burnished red; Avoncrisp (Cr) crispy and disease- and bolt-resistant; Valdor (Cr) large, crisp, rounded heads; Imperial Winter (B) large, tender hearts; Premier (B) large, firm, rounded hearts; May Queen (B) good hearts, red-tinged leaves.

SITE AND SOIL

Some of the cos lettuces seem to grow quite well in light shade, but most varieties appreciate the sun on their leaves. Choose a patch of ground that was manured for a previous crop and apply lime a month or two before sowing if the soil is acid. Two weeks before sowing scatter two handfuls of a general fertiliser over each square metre (yard) of ground and hoe it in.

SEED SOWING

Whether the crops are sown under cloches or in the open the drills should be 1cm (½in) deep and the seeds should be sown thinly. I don't like transplanting lettuce – often it leads to bolting (running to seed) – so I prefer to sow *in situ* and thin out the seedlings so that they grow on with no check. Allow 30cm (1ft) between lettuce rows, unless you want to cram two under a row of wide cloches, in which case cut the spacing down to 18 or 20cm (7 or 8in). Sow summer lettuce at fortnightly intervals, half a row at a time. Entire rows of lettuce maturing at once will provide you with an embarrassing and useless glut. Thin the plants within the row to 20cm (8in) for cos varieties, 15cm (6in) for Salad Bowl, and 25cm (10in) for butterhead and crisphead types.

CULTIVATION

Try to keep the soil evenly moist at all times. It's not easy I know, but a very dry spell can lead to bolting. Hoe regularly between the rows and pull off any damaged or rotting leaves as soon as you see them. Trap slugs continuously (see page 133). Ventilate crops under cloches in reasonable weather. Feed winter lettuce in March by scattering a light dusting of a general fertiliser alongside the row and hoeing it in.

HARVESTING

Pull the lettuces as soon as you consider them usable; leave them too long and they'll turn bitter before running to seed. Remove all the plant and put the dirty lower leaves and the stalk on the compost heap – don't leave them on the soil around the other lettuces. Lettuce won't store, but careful sowing will ensure you a succession of fresh crops.

PESTS AND DISEASES

Aphids, slugs, birds and rabbits can attack your lettuces and botrytis and mildew are the worst diseases – particularly in late summer and through the winter.

IN BRIEF

Site and soil Open sunny spot; reasonably rich and well-drained soil that is not too acid

Sowing and harvesting chart

Sow	Cloches on/	Cloches off	Harvest	Varieties
Late February/ early March	2 weeks before sowing	Early May	Late May June	Winter Density, Unrivalled, Tom Thumb, Little Gem
Mid-March/ mid-June	–		June/August	Barcarolle, Webb's Wonderful, Salad Bowl
Late June/ late July	Late September	After harvesting	September/ December	Avondefiance, Continuity, Avoncrisp
Late August/ early September	–	–	May/June	Valdor, Imperial Winter, Winter Density
October	2 weeks before sowing	After harvesting	Late March/ May	Unrivalled, Premier, May Queen

Successional sowing interval 2 weeks (for summer crops)
Effort* (summer crops) ** (winter crops)

SHOW TIPS

Grow as recommended taking extra care over watering and pest control. Keep the plants free of slugs, caterpillars and aphids which will ruin your chances on the showbench as well as on the table. Cut the plants as near to show time as possible so that they remain fresh and crisp. They should have large, firm but tender hearts and be of a good, unblemished colour. The outer leaves should not be limp. Webb's Wonderful is a reliable old variety and Lakeland a promising newcomer. In the cos class try Barcarolle or Lobjoit's Green Cos.

MARROW & COURGETTE

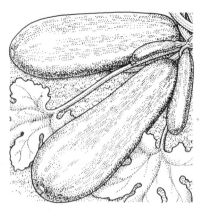

Stuffed marrows and fried courgettes are two of the highlights of summer. Neither is difficult to grow provided you are generous with the manure and the weather is generous with the sun.

VARIETIES

Let's make it clear from the start that courgettes are just immature marrows – leave them to grow on the plant and most of them will turn into whoppers. Courgette fans need look no further than Zucchini (for green fruits) and Golden Zucchini (for yellow fruits). Green Bush is, I think, the best marrow – especially in its 'Improved' variety. It takes up far less room than the trailing type of marrow which is rather a nuisance with its habit of roaming the plot. If you are really mean buy one packet of Zucchini seeds and let some plants produce marrows and others courgettes.

SITE AND SOIL

It's not a bad idea to reserve a patch of soil that can be used for your marrows and courgettes year after year. It should be in a sunny but sheltered part of the plot and dug over each winter or spring when lashings of well-rotted garden compost, manure and a scattering of fertiliser can be worked into the top 30cm (1ft) of soil.

SEED SOWING

You can sow the seeds outdoors where they are to grow if you wait until late May, but often they fail to come to much. Sow them instead in late April in a pot of peat-based potting compost and germinate them in the airing cupboard or on a warm windowsill where they can be covered with a polythene bag. Sow two seeds in each 8-cm (3-in) pot and thin to one if both grow. Gradually harden them off before planting out in late May or early June.

PLANTING

Water the plants well before planting them out. Plant with a trowel so that the surface of the compost in the pot is level with the surface of the soil outside. Space the plants 60cm (2ft) apart on the square and water them in. Protect them with cloches for a week or two if possible. Set up slug traps immediately or scatter pellets among the plants regularly. Summer watering will be made easier if the plants are planted in shallow hollows in the soil.

CULTIVATION

Apply copious amounts of water in summer – never let the soil get the slightest bit dry. In late June lay a thick mulch of organic matter around each plant when the soil is moist. Feed fortnightly with a diluted liquid tomato fertiliser from early July onwards. If the weather is cool at flowering time then help out with pollination. Remove a male flower (the one with a thin stalk) and strip off the petals before pushing it into the centre of the female (the one with a miniature marrow for a flower stalk). When marrows start to form place a flat piece of wood under each fruit to prevent it from being attacked by slugs and fungus diseases.

To ensure a decent crop of marrows, pollinate each female flower (the one with a mini-marrow behind it) by pushing a male flower (petals removed) into its centre.

HARVESTING

Cut courgettes regularly to keep the plants cropping. Cut marrows when they are large enough to use.

STORAGE

Marrows can be stored on shelves in a cold but frost-proof shed or garage where they will keep for weeks. Cut them in September before the frosts. Eat up your courgettes as soon as possible.

PESTS AND DISEASES

Slugs are the main pest; grey mould, mildew and mosaic are the diseases to watch out for. Lack of food and sunshine may result in the production of few female flowers.

SHOW TIPS

Marrows are usually shown in pairs, so aim to produce two that are evenly matched unless you are going for the 'biggest in show' class. Grow as recommended and try to obtain fruits that are shapely, evenly formed and evenly coloured. Support the fruits so that they do not rest on the soil during their development. As soon as one fruit reaches the required size and plumpness it can be cut and stored in a cool place for a few days while its companion catches up. But beware of storing it for too long, for freshness is a quality the judges will be looking for. Suitable varieties are Green Bush and Table Dainty. For the whopper class, Long Green Trailing is usually grown. It should be planted on top of a mound of solid, well-rotted manure, topped with a little soil. Feed it weekly in summer and never let it run short of water. Allow just one fruit to form and keep excessive stem growth trimmed back so that the plant's energies are concentrated

IN BRIEF

Site and soil Warm, sunny spot; very rich and moisture-retentive soil
Sow Late April indoors
Plant Late May or early June
Successional sowing Unnecessary
Harvest July to September
Effort **

on swelling the fruit. Some growers thread a strand of wool (or shoelace) through the stem of the fruit with a needle and trail the wool into a jar of sugar and water. The plant supposedly draws in the sugar and fattens up. Try it if you want; I've never been desperate enough!

ONION

Easy to grow and easy to store, onions are one of the most reliable vegetable crops. Grow several kinds to make sure of a succession of bulbs.

VARIETIES
Ailsa Craig and Bedfordshire Champion are the two all-time greats to grow as maincrop onions from seeds. Express Yellow O-X and Imai Early Yellow are well-tried Japanese varieties. For autumn sowings of traditional varieties use Ailsa Craig or Reliance. For good spring onions look no further than White Lisbon, and for pickling The Queen or Paris Silver Skin will stay crunchy and reasonably white. Sturon and Stuttgarter Giant are varieties of onion set that I have grown successfully, and Unwin's First Early is the variety to plant in autumn.

SITE AND SOIL
All onions need sun to ripen them off and prolong their storage life so pick an open, unshaded spot. Well-drained soil is essential and all ground should be limed in autumn if it is acid and well-cultivated during the winter before sowing or planting. (Avoid growing onions on the same site every year – it can lead to serious outbreaks of disease.) Work in plenty of well-rotted garden compost or manure and then let the soil settle for several months so that the enrichment is well broken down by the time the crop is started off. Scatter two handfuls of blood, bone and fishmeal over each square metre (yard) of ground three weeks before sowing and lightly rake this into the surface.

SEED SOWING
Avoid transplanting onions if possible – they tend to run to seed if their growth is checked. Instead, sow them where they are to mature and thin out the young plants to a suitable spacing. Before sowing make sure that the soil is really well-worked with a rake so that the surface is friable but not too dusty. Never sow in a

cold spell. The drills should be 1cm (½in) deep and 30cm (1ft) apart and the seeds sown thinly. Spring onion and pickling onion rows can be as close as 23cm (9in). Thin the larger bulb onions to 10 to 15cm (4 or 6in). Spring onions can be thinned gradually and the thinnings eaten. Pickling onions need no thinning. Autumn-sown onions (which are a risky crop in exposed areas) are thinned once in autumn to 2.5-cm (1-in) spacings, and finally in spring to 10cm (4in) when they have come through their ordeal.

PLANTING

Onion sets (small bulbs) are very convenient and are preferred to seeds by many gardeners. 225g (½lb) of sets will plant up a 10.5-m (35-ft) row. Plant them with a trowel so that just the tips are visible above the soil and space the bulbs 10cm (4in) apart. Replant any that lift themselves out or are dislodged by birds or worms. The ease of growing sets may outweigh the fact that their matured bulbs are smaller than those grown from seeds; indeed some cooks may prefer smaller bulbs. In my experience there is no problem with storing properly ripened onions grown from sets.

CULTIVATION

Hoe regularly between the rows and hand weed between the plants. Apply plenty of water to maincrop onions between April and June if the soil shows signs of

becoming very dry. Cut off any flowerheads as soon as they are noticed and earmark these bulbs for early use – they will not store. Occasional liquid feeds are very much appreciated. When the foliage of maincrop onions starts to turn yellow in mid-summer do not apply any more water – instead let the bulbs dry off. The leaves will fall over and can be tidied by laying them so that those of two adjacent rows are both folded towards one another. During August, lift the bulbs with a fork and leave them on the surface of the soil to dry off. If the

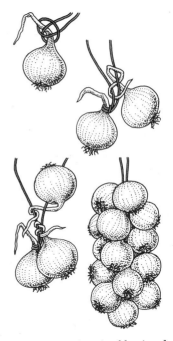

You can store onions in old pairs of tights, but they don't look as romantic and French as when they're knotted into ropes.

Once your onions are a good size and the time has come to ripen them, bend over their tops so that the sun can get at the bulbs.

weather is very wet, cover the bulbs with cloches or remove them to a frame to dry off. Damp and unripened bulbs will store badly and may even rot away. Autumn-sown onions left to over-winter in the ground will normally have to manage without any protection, but overwintering spring onions can be cloched in September and decloched in March. Remember that autumn-sown and autumn-planted onions do not store well – they should be used as soon as possible when they are ripe.

STORAGE

When they have been allowed to dry off for a couple of weeks, maincrop bulb onions can be knotted into ropes or trimmed of their foliage and stored in old pairs of tights hung up in a cool, dry, well-lit place. Stored in the dark onions will sprout.

PESTS AND DISEASES

Eelworm and onion fly are the two major pests and mildew, white rot and neck rot are the most common diseases.

IN BRIEF

Site and soil A sunny spot is essential. The soil should be rich and limed if it is acid

Sow March or April – maincrop varieties for storing; mid-August – Japanese varieties for early summer harvesting; mid-August – selected varieties for earlier ripening than maincrop sowing; March to August – spring onions; April – pickling onions

Plant March or April – onion sets (small bulbs); September to November – special overwintering onion sets

Successional sowing Only necessary for spring onions – sow portions of a row at monthly intervals

Harvest August onwards – maincrop; Late June – Japanese varieties; Late July – selected autumn-sown varieties; May to March – spring onions; August – pickling onions; August onwards – maincrop onions from sets; June/July onwards – overwintering sets

Effort *

SHALLOT

These miniature onions are sweetly flavoured and valued by discerning cooks. Plant them like onion sets but in February or March. Set them 15cm (6in) apart in rows 30cm (1ft) apart. By July each bulb will have made a cluster of bulbs which can be harvested, dried and stored for cooking during autumn and winter. Retain a few firm bulbs for planting next year.

GARLIC

Grow garlic from 'cloves' exactly as you would onions from sets, but find the warmest, sunniest spot you can. Lift and store the bulbs in August. In good summers you will harvest a good supply – in miserable summers your yield may be more disappointing.

SHOW TIPS

The expert onion growers use the same bed year after year, enriching it greatly with manure each autumn. Seed is sown traditionally on Christmas Day (if you've nothing better to do) under glass. Ailsa Craig and Bedfordshire Champion will do for most exhibitors, but if you are going for the largest possible onions then you need Robinson's Mammoth Improved Onion or Kelsae. Prick out and grow on the plants and plant them out in the prepared soil in late April. Space the plants 30cm (1ft) apart in both directions. Never let the soil dry out. Apply a little general fertiliser between the rows in June. Three weeks before the show date, go along the rows and pull off any damaged outer skins so that the clean one left behind will have time to colour up well before the show. Bend over the onion tops and prise free the bulbs to allow them to ripen in time. Lift and dry off the plants two or three days before showing, and the day before, cut off the roots and also the leaves. Tie down the 5-cm (2-in) leaf-stalk base with fine twine so that it makes a neat finish. Judges will look for firm, good-sized onions with thin necks and few blemishes. They do not like to see that the bulbs have been peeled free of damaged layers, so make sure that you do this cleaning-up operation well in advance as recommended.

PARSNIP

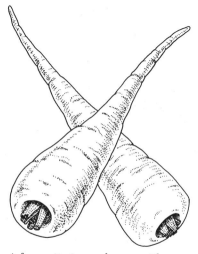

A favourite in our house with winter roasts, parsnips are easy to grow in well-cultivated soil and they last well through the winter with no special storage.

VARIETIES
Tender and True and Hollow Crown Improved are both tasty and reliable.

SITE AND SOIL
Although they appreciate an open, sunny spot best, parsnips are not a bad choice for that corner of the plot that is partially shaded by trees. They insist on a well-culti-vated soil if their roots are not to fork, and they prefer ground which has been manured for a previous crop. Dig over the soil during the autumn before sowing. Lime the ground in winter if it is acid, and scatter one handful of a general fertiliser over each square metre (yard) one week before sowing and lightly rake it in.

SEED SOWING
Take out 2.5-cm (1-in) deep drills 30cm (1ft) apart and sow three seeds every 10cm (4in) along the row. Thin to leave the strongest plant at each station as the seed-lings grow. Germination is rather slow so don't be impatient.

CULTIVATION
Hoe regularly between the rows and give the ground a thorough soaking in prolonged dry spells.

HARVESTING
Lift the roots when they are large enough to use. There is no need to lift and store them through the winter – they are bone hardy and can be left in the soil until March if necessary. Mark the rows with sticks (the foliage dies down and makes location difficult).

STORAGE
If frosty or snowy weather is fore-cast, lift a few roots and store them in dry sand for easier access. Lift all remaining roots in March and heel in on a corner of the plot (see leeks, page 81).

PESTS AND DISEASES
Canker is the most troublesome problem with parsnips. Carrot fly and celery fly may occasionally attack. The roots may crack open when heavy rains follow a period of drought.

SHOW TIPS
Long, evenly tapering roots are

required here, and there is no finer way of achieving these than inserting 60-cm (2-ft) lengths of 10- or 12-cm (4- or 5-in) diameter

Grow your show parsnips individually in sunken lengths of drainpipe filled with sifted soil – they'll be much longer than if grown in unprepared earth.

plastic drainpipe into the ground, and filling these with old potting compost or a mixture of equal parts sieved garden soil, peat and sand with a little fertiliser added. Alternatively use the crowbar method. Ram an iron bar into the ground to a depth of 60cm (2ft), wiggle it round to make a conical hole and fill this with the recommended mixture. Sow three seeds on top of each prepared site in March, and thin to leave the strongest. Water well during the growing season and lift carefully before the show. Wash the roots and choose those that are even, smooth-skinned, white and free from any blemishes. The shoulders should be well defined. Trim off any side roots. Tender and True is a popular show variety.

IN BRIEF

Site and soil Preferably open and sunny, though light shade is tolerated; good, well-cultivated soil that is not too rich. Lime very acid soils.
Sow Late February (in mild winters) to May
Successional sowing Unnecessary
Harvest September to March
Effort *

PEA

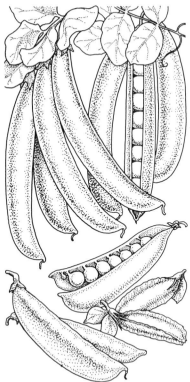

The early peas are as highly prized as new potatoes, but it takes careful planning to ensure that the supply is extended through the summer. Work out your succession at the start of the season.

VARIETIES

For those first sowings under cloches choose Little Marvel, Hurst Beagle (very tasty) or Feltham First – all at 45cm (1½ft). March to June sowings of Hurst Green Shaft 75cm (2½ft), Kelvedon Wonder 45cm (1½ft) and Lud 1m (3ft) will yield fine-flavoured crops. Choose Kelvedon Wonder again for summer sowings, and Meteor 45cm (1½ft) for autumn sowings under cloches. **Mange-tous** Mange-tous peas are also sown from March - June but their pods are picked and cooked whole before the peas fatten. They are deliciously tender

and tasty. A variety called Sugar Snap 2m (6ft) produces fat pods which are crisp and fleshy. They are cooked like ordinary peas.

SITE AND SOIL

Peas like plenty of sun, though they will put up with just a modicum of shade in the heart of summer. Their roots are greedy so prepare the soil well. If the ground is acid apply lime in autumn and in winter dig over the soil and work in as much well-rotted garden compost or manure as possible. Break down the surface of the soil with a fork two weeks before sowing and work in three handfuls of a general fertiliser to each square metre (yard). Although peas need a well-drained soil they do not enjoy drought – treat them like gluttons to get the best crops.

SEED SOWING

Never sow peas when the earth is cold and wet – they will simply rot away. Wait until a mild spell when the soil is not soggy and then take out a flat-bottomed drill 5cm (2in) deep and 15cm (6in) wide. Space sow the seeds 5cm (2in) apart – rather closer for the earliest sowings so that the birds and mice can have a nibble without ruining your crop. Replace and firm the soil with the back of a rake. You can sow peas in 'V'-shaped drills but the flat-bottomed type produce more pods per metre of row. The distance between rows should be equivalent to the ultimate height of the crop (see above), but smaller vegetables such as radishes, lettuces and spring onions can be grown between rows of peas. For the earliest crops the cloches should be put in position two weeks before sowing. Remove them as soon as the plants hit the glass. Cloches over the autumn-sown crops can be removed in early May – stand them on bricks if the plants need more headroom before this date.

CULTIVATION

In spite of what some folk say, all peas need to be supported. As soon as they are 8cm (3in) high, push twiggy branches among them or surround them with a fence of canes and string. Hoe between the rows and really soak the soil in

However dwarf your peas are supposed to be, they'll still fall over unless you stake them. I find brushwood the easiest stuff to use, but canes and string are a substitute if twigs are hard to find.

dry weather. Where bird damage is a problem, cover the rows of seeds with tunnels of wire netting and later protect the maturing pods with plastic netting which can be laid over the plants more easily. A late spring mulch of well-rotted organic matter can boost yields – apply it when the soil is moist. Cloche autumn-maturing crops in early September.

HARVESTING

Pick the pods as soon as they are well filled. Never allow them to stand on the plant too long or they will harden and cropping will stop. Cut off the plants leaving their nitrogen-producing roots in the soil when harvesting is over.

STORAGE

Peas freeze well.

PESTS AND DISEASES

Pea moth, pea and bean weevil, birds, mice, slugs, thrips and aphids are the likely pests. Mildew and damping off are the common diseases. Don't worry – they won't all attack your crop!

SHOW TIPS

Sow in 'V'-shaped drills, spacing the seeds 10cm (4in) apart. Grow as recommended paying particular attention to watering at flowering time and after. Mulch with well-rotted compost or grass clippings in June. Peas are the very devil to time, so sow part of a row at weekly intervals over a four-week period from mid-May to mid-June for an August show. Take precautions to prevent pest attack – especially thrips which will disfigure the pods, and pea moth which produces maggoty peas. Suitable varieties include Hurst Green Shaft and Alderman, though the latter grows to 1.5m (5ft) and needs tall stakes. Cut the pods carefully, handling them by their stalks so that the bloom is not rubbed off. Hold them against a table lamp to see if they are full of fat peas. The judges will look for large, well-filled pods of a fresh colour with undisturbed bloom. No blemishes or pest attack should be visible.

IN BRIEF

Site and soil Bright and sunny spot; rich, well-drained but moisture-retentive soil

Sow Late February/mid-March – under cloches; Late March/mid-June – in the open; Late June/mid-July – in the open for autumn crop; October/November – under cloches for spring harvesting

Successional sowing interval 3 weeks

Harvest Late May/June – early clochéd sowings; Early July/September – spring and early summer sowings; October/November – summer sowings; May – autumn sowings

Effort **

POTATO

An essential choice for most plots, new potatoes are among the most highly appreciated of vegetables. Grow the maincrop varieties if you have room to spare or a piece of ground that needs a good working over.

VARIETIES

Good flavour and a fair yield are the qualities I look for in a potato variety, but disease resistance is also a valuable attribute. These are the varieties I would recommend to do well on most soils and in most situations.
Earlies: Maris Bard (waxy), Epicure (floury); **second earlies**: Vanessa (waxy), Catriona (floury); **maincrop**: Golden Wonder (floury), Desiree (waxy).

SITE AND SOIL

Spuds will really grow on any soil, but the best yields are produced on fairly rich ground which has been dug and manured in the autumn and winter previous to planting. Avoid frost pockets where the young leaves may be burnt off in spring. First-time gardeners are often told to grow potatoes to clean up new ground. It is the earthing up and soil cultivation in general that does the trick, not some magic ingredient of the potato tuber!

PREPARING TO PLANT

Potatoes sold for planting (rather than eating) are called seed potatoes, and they should be certified free of virus diseases which can seriously reduce yields. Buy the tubers in February. A 3kg (7lb) bag will plant up a 9-m (10-yd) row of earlies, or a 14-m (15-yd) row of second earlies or maincrop potatoes. As soon as you have bought the tubers, remove them from the bag and arrange them in seed trays or egg trays so that the ends which possess the most buds or 'eyes' point uppermost. Stand the trays in a well-lit place that is cool but frost-proof. Slowly the buds will begin to grow, and when they are about 2.5cm (1in) long the potatoes will be ready to plant. This shoot-inducing operation is known as 'chitting' and it generally hastens cropping and also improves the yield.

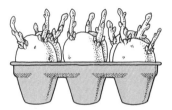

You'll get a better, earlier crop from your spuds if you sprout or 'chit' them before planting. Arrange them 'eyes' uppermost in egg trays in a light, frostproof place. They'll be ready for planting about six weeks later when the sprouts are 2.5cm (1in) or so high.

Some gardeners remove all but three of the shoots on each potato; I've never bothered. Nor have I been mean enough to cut up large tubers into two pieces, each of which possesses one or two shoots. Some money can be saved by doing this, but there is a greater chance that the plants may be attacked by fungus disease or infected with viruses from an unsterilised knife.

PLANTING

Plant when the soil is moist but not sodden. Use a trowel (it saves taking out a deep drill) and plant each tuber, shoots uppermost, so that it is covered with 5cm (2in) of soil. Plant earlies 30cm (1ft) apart; second earlies and maincrop varieties 45cm (1½ft) apart – they produce more tubers and so need more space. Rows of earlies should be 45cm (1½ft) apart; the rest 60cm (2ft) apart. After planting rake a little blood, bone and fishmeal into the surface of the soil at the rate of two handfuls to each 1-m (1-yd) run of row.

CULTIVATION
Pull soil around the shoots as soon as they appear to protect them from frost. Earth up like this if the weather continues cold, but otherwise wait until the tops are 15cm (6in) high before pulling soil up around them so that only the tips are visible. One good earthing up like this will be quite sufficient to prevent the tubers from turning green (and so becoming inedible). There is no need to earth up the rows madly right through the summer unless you want the exercise and need to smother rampant weed growth. In late spring make sure that the soil never dries out.

HARVESTING
Earlies will be ready in June or July – flowering is a good indication that the tubers are just about ready. Lift a sample root and make a spot check. Lift the tubers as you need them. Second early and maincrop varieties will follow on. On no account eat the green tomato-like fruits which may appear after the flowers – they are very poisonous.

STORAGE
Lift any remaining tubers in October, allow them to dry off for a few hours on the soil surface and then store them in thick paper sacks in a cool but frostproof place. They should be kept in the dark if they are not to sprout, and only undamaged tubers should be stored. Many folk enjoy new potatoes at Christmas and this is simple to achieve if you bury some tubers in a tin of moist sand immediately after lifting in late June or early July. Mark the site of the tin so that you can locate it on the morning of December 25th.

PESTS AND DISEASES
Slugs, eelworm and wireworms are the pests that may be encountered. Scab, wart disease, blight and virus diseases may also attack.

SHOW TIPS
Incorporate plenty of compost during winter digging. In February scatter 85g of potato fertiliser (15:15:21) over each square metre (3oz per square yard). Plant mid-March on 5cm (2in) compost in 15-cm (6-in) deep 'U'-shaped drills. Allow 45cm (18in) between tubers and 75cm (30in) between rows. Choose 85g (3oz) size certified seed potatoes with three to four sprouts. Cover with 10cm (4in) sieved loam or peat. Ridge up in May after spreading 55g (2oz) fertiliser along each metre (yard) of row. During tuber formation in June water frequently. Apply fortnightly anti-blight sprays from early July. Show undamaged,

---

IN BRIEF

Site and soil The best crops grow in an open, sunny spot on ground which has been well enriched the previous autumn and winter; avoid frost pockets

Plant Mid- to late March – early varieties; April – second early and maincrop varieties

Harvest Mid-June to July – earlies; August onwards – second earlies and maincrop

Effort **

uniformly medium-sized tubers of good shape with few eyes. Wash them and avoid damaging the skin which should be as clear as possible. Suitable varieties for showing include: Maris Peer, Pentland Javelin, Catriona, Desiree, Vanessa.

PUMPKIN

More a flower show novelty than a bread-and-butter crop, but one that makes a good pie and a good talking point.

VARIETIES
Nearly all the prizewinners are Hundredweight (which is a bit of an exaggeration but not much)!

SITE AND SOIL
In the dappled shade of a tree or in the open – pumpkins will thrive in either situation provided the soil is rich. In early spring dig a hole 1m (1yd) square and one spit (spade blade) deep and fill it with well-rotted compost or manure. Spread a 15-cm (6-in) layer of soil on top of the enrichment and tread it firm. Pumpkins need plenty of room, so don't grow them unless you have space to spare.

SEED SOWING
Sow the seeds individually in peat pots containing a peat-based potting compost. Start them off in a warm airing cupboard or on a windowsill in April, or alternatively, plant three seeds outdoors where a plant is to grow in May. The former is the more reliable method, but if you prefer the latter, cover the site with a cloche and thin to one seedling when the young plants are 8cm (3in) high.

PLANTING
Plant in late May or early June, soaking the compost and peat pot beforehand. Do not plant too deeply. Water the youngster in thoroughly.

CULTIVATION
Never allow the plant to go short of water. Apply liquid feeds once a week. Hand weed around the plant. Pinch the shoot tip out when eight leaves have formed. Arrange the long shoots so that they do not interfere with other crops. Remove all but four developing pumpkins, or all but one if you want a mammoth.

HARVESTING
Wait until the first frosts kill off the leaves before you cut the fruit and bring it indoors.

STORAGE
Wipe the pumpkin clean and store it on a shelf or in a string bag at a

---

IN BRIEF

Site and soil Sunny or slightly shady spot; very, very rich soil
Sow April indoors; May in the open
Plant Late May/early June
Successional sowing Unnecessary
Harvest September
Effort **

temperature of around 15°C (60°F). Chefs cook pumpkin in a variety of ways, the simplest of which is to boil it in a minimum of water after which it is served as an ordinary vegetable. It can also be put in pies, roasted around the joint or turned into soup or jam.

PESTS AND DISEASES
As for marrow (see page 85).

SHOW TIPS
Grow as for large marrows.

RADISH

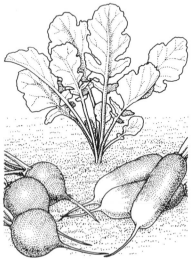

The quickest growing crop of all and one that is best squeezed in between taller vegetables utilising space that would otherwise be wasted.

VARIETIES
I admit to being a real stick-in-the-mud when it comes to choosing radishes. I still grow the rosy and spherical Cherry Belle which I first bought at the local ironmongers at the age of 10. French Breakfast is an ancient alternative if you prefer longer roots. Saxerre is one of the best for the early cloched sowings, and Round Red Forcing is also worth recommending. Winter radishes are larger altogether and will stand in the soil for months without spoiling. China Rose is red with white flesh, and Black Spanish is black with white flesh. The last-named is available in both globe and long-rooted forms.

SITE AND SOIL
Ground which was manured for a previous crop is best. It should be well worked, well drained and not poverty stricken. Radishes will happily put up with a little shade cast by taller crops. Use them as gap fillers to make barren strips productive. Rake a light dusting of blood, bone and fishmeal into the strip of soil a week before sowing.

SEED SOWING
Sow only when the soil is moist but not when it is cold and soggy. Put cloches in position two weeks before sowing the earliest crops and keep them in position until the roots are harvested (ventilating when necessary). Sow a section of a row at fortnightly intervals. The drills should be 1cm (½in) deep. Radishes fail to develop properly unless they are quickly thinned. Thin ordinary varieties to 2.5cm (1in) and winter radishes to 15cm (6in). If you want to grow more than one row, space them 30cm (1ft) apart; summer radishes 15cm (6in) apart.

CULTIVATION
Never let the plants go short of water or they will become woody. Soak the soil around them in dry spells. The secret of growing good radishes is to make them develop quickly. Hoe regularly between the rows and hand weed between the plants in the case of winter radishes.

HARVESTING AND STORAGE
Pull ordinary radishes as soon as they are of an edible size. Winter radishes can stay in the soil until they are needed or they can be

lifted in late autumn, their tops cut off and the roots stored in boxes of sand kept in a cool shed or garage. Eat ordinary radishes whole; the winter type grated or sliced.

PESTS AND DISEASES
Flea beetles may attack the seedlings.

SHOW TIPS
Grow as recommended, sowing from mid-June to early July. Select plump, fresh roots that are of a uniform size. Retain the foliage and tie the radishes in a bundle. The colour should be bright and the washed roots should be free from blemishes. The flesh should be tender – not woody. Avoid any radishes that are showing flower stems and any over 2.5cm (1in) in diameter.

IN BRIEF

Site and soil   A well-drained and well worked soil that is not too poor; a little shade is tolerated
Sow   February – under cloches; March to August – in the open; July and August – winter radish in the open
Successional sowing interval   2 weeks (sow sections of a row)
Harvest   April to September; October to March – winter radish
Effort   *

RHUBARB

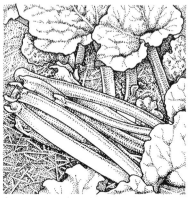

Poor old rhubarb is often relegated to an out-of-the-way corner where it has to struggle to grow. Don't be mean – give it a spot in the sun, plant it in rich earth and it will keep you in puddings for months.

VARIETIES
Until recently it seemed that time had stood still in the rhubarb world and we were still using ancient varieties. There are those gardeners who will not part with their Champagne, Holstein Blood Red and Early Albert, but I would urge them to have a go with the new Cawood Delight or Cawood Castle which are extremely vigorous, very tasty and good looking when bottled.

SITE AND SOIL
The average household needs only a small rhubarb bed consisting of perhaps five or six plants. Site these along one end of the plot where they will not overshadow other crops but where they will get plenty of sun. Dig over the soil in autumn and winter working in generous amounts of well-rotted garden compost or manure. The soil must be well drained.

PLANTING
Rhubarb can be raised from seed but it's time-consuming and far better to buy a few plants of a variety that is known to perform well. Plant the 'crowns' 5cm (2in) below the surface of the prepared soil and 1m (3ft) apart in March. Use a spade to plant and firm the soil around the roots with your feet.

CULTIVATION

Don't harvest any stalks in the first year; instead let the plants build up their strength. Cut off any flowers that form and remove any weed growth around the plants. Each February spread a layer of compost or manure around each plant to give it a boost. Lift, divide and replant every four or five years.

FORCING

Plants can be forced outdoors occasionally with no detriment to their health. Cover one crown

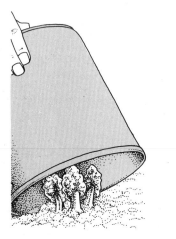

Covered with a straw-stuffed bucket in January, a fat crown of rhubarb should be yielding some succulent sticks by March.

with a large straw-filled wooden box or bucket in January and keep it snug and warm until March when some tender pink sticks should be ready for harvesting. Give the plant a rest for the rest of the year, applying a monthly liquid feed from April to July to build up its strength again. Do not force the same plant the following year.

HARVESTING

Pull the sticks from unforced plants as soon as they are large enough to use. Start with the outer sticks and work inwards spreading your harvest evenly over all the plants. Stop pulling in July and let the leaves die down over the plants in autumn.

STORAGE

Rhubarb freezes well and can also be bottled, pickled or jammed.

PESTS AND DISEASES

Crown rot and honey fungus are the only likely problems.

SHOW TIPS

Grow as recommended, being generous with the soil preparation and applying fortnightly liquid feeds through the summer. Select long, straight sticks for showing. They should be fresh and tender, reasonably thick and of a good red colouring. Trim off all except the lower 5cm (2in) of the leaf and tie the sticks in a neat bundle.

IN BRIEF

Site and soil Sunny spot; rich, well-cultivated soil
Plant March
Harvest April to July (March if forced)
Effort *

SALSIFY & SCORZONERA

Two long-rooted vegetables for the connoisseur. Try half a row of each; they make a change from carrots!

VARIETIES
Salsify is called the vegetable oyster and consequently tempts many gardeners with ideas above their station. Several varieties are offered: Mammoth, Sandwich Island and Giant should all perform reasonably well. Scorzonera is not so popular because its name is hard to pronounce! Russian Giant is the most widely available variety, but Long Black is also offered – take your pick.

SITE AND SOIL
With roots about 30cm (1ft) long, these vegetables really insist on a deeply worked soil that offers no obstacles to downward movement. Dig it well in autumn and winter but do not work in any compost or manure or the roots will fork. Land manured for a previous crop is fine. Sun is enjoyed, so pick an open spot. Immediately before sowing, lightly dust the soil with blood, bone and fishmeal and rake it into the surface.

SEED SOWING
Sow the seeds in drills 2.5cm (1in) deep and 30cm (1ft) apart. Thin the resulting seedlings first to 8cm (3in) and then to 15cm (6in).

CULTIVATION
Hoe regularly between the rows. Soak the soil around the plants in dry spells.

HARVESTING
Leave the roots in the ground until you are ready to use them. Cover the rows with straw or bracken to give a little frost protection.

STORAGE
In heavy soils, or where winter harvesting will be difficult, the roots can all be lifted in October, trimmed of their foliage and stored in boxes of dry sand in a frostproof shed or garage. Both roots are tasty if scrubbed and boiled. Don't peel the roots or you'll remove most of the flesh and the flavour. The skin of scorzonera will slip off easily after cooking.

PESTS AND DISEASES
None to speak of.

IN BRIEF

Site and soil   Sunny spot; well-cultivated but not freshly manured soil. Grow poorly on stony ground.
Sow   April and May
Successional sowing   Unnecessary
Harvest   September to April – scorzonera; October to April – salsify
Effort   *

SPINACH

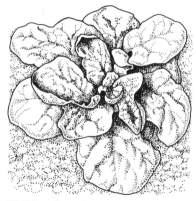

Children hate it; many grown-ups love it, but whatever your feelings you cannot deny that spinach is a valuable gap filler which can be cropped all the year round.

VARIETIES
The following are among the best varieties of their type:**Summer spinach**: Longstanding Round, Norvak;**Winter spinach**: Longstanding Prickly, Broad-leaved Prickly (the 'prickly' and 'round' refer to the seeds, not the leaves); **Perpetual spinach** (Spinach beet): sold simply as 'Perpetual Spinach'

SITE AND SOIL
The two types of ordinary spinach sown for summer or winter use like sun and a rich soil; perpetual spinach also likes a generous diet but it will put up with dry soils and a little shade. Lime very acid ground at least a month before it is dug and manured in readiness for the crop. Allow it a month to settle before sowing. Dust the ground with a general fertiliser about a week before sowing.

SEED SOWING
Sow the seeds in 2.5-cm (1-in) deep drills, spacing them 8cm (3in) apart. Allow 30cm (1ft) between rows. Thin the resulting seedlings to 23cm (9in) if they are for winter use; to 30cm (1ft) if they are for summer use.

CULTIVATION
Soak the soil around the plants when it shows signs of drying out. Hoe between the rows regularly. Cut off any flowerheads that form. Winter-maturing spinach will stay in better condition if it is covered with cloches in October.

HARVESTING
Pull the leaves as soon as they are large enough to use. Spread your harvesting over all the plants, taking the outer leaves first.

STORAGE
Spinach can be cooked and frozen.

PESTS AND DISEASES
Slugs and birds may be a problem. Bolting may be caused by drought and lack of nutrients. Downy mildew sometimes strikes.

IN BRIEF

Site and soil   Open sunny site; rich, well-drained soil
Sow   March to May – summer spinach; August to September – winter spinach; March to April – perpetual spinach for summer and autumn use; July to August – perpetual spinach for winter use
Harvest   May to November – summer spinach; November to March – winter spinach; June to mid-winter – perpetual spinach (first sowing); November to May – perpetual spinach (second sowing)
Effort   *

SWEDE

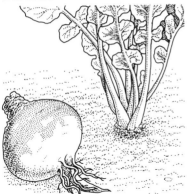

An easy-to-grow root that is a must on the vegetable plot. It matures in autumn and winter and is delectable mashed up and mixed in with potatoes, or boiled, buttered and peppered.

VARIETIES
Marian is the best choice. It is tasty, reliable and resistant to clubroot and mildew. Mancunian Bronze Top and Acme are older but still fairly reliable varieties.

SITE AND SOIL
Choose a sunny part of the plot which was manured for a previous crop. Dig it well in the winter and a week before sowing scatter two handfuls of a general fertiliser over each square metre (yard) of ground. Do not grow your swedes on land previously occupied by brassicas for they can also suffer from clubroot. Lime very acid soil before it is dug.

SEED SOWING
Sow the seeds thinly in 1cm (½in) deep drills spaced 38cm (15in) apart. Thin the resulting seedlings quite quickly – first to 8cm (3in), then to 23cm (9in).

CULTIVATION
Make sure the soil around the plants never gets really dry – soak it in prolonged sunny spells. Hoe between the rows and hand weed between the plants.

HARVESTING AND STORAGE
Pull the roots from October onwards as soon as they are large enough to use. They may be left in the ground through the winter and pulled as needed, or in November, they can be lifted, trimmed of their leaves and the sound roots stored in boxes of dry sand. Keep them in a cool but frostproof place.

PESTS AND DISEASES
Flea beetle is the commonest pest, and clubroot and brown heart are the most likely diseases.

IN BRIEF

Site and soil Open sunny site; well-drained soil manured for a previous crop
Sow May to June
Successional sowing Unnecessary
Harvest October to March
Effort *

SWEET CORN

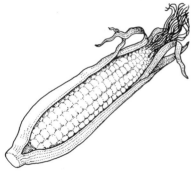

Although it does best in the milder counties, sweet corn is worth a try even in the frozen north where, if it is started early, it will produce enough mouth-watering cobs to make the gamble worthwhile.

VARIETIES

I always grow John Innes Hybrid which gives a superb tasty crop relatively early in the season. Northern gardeners might like to compare its speed of ripening with First of All which a friend in the Midlands swears by as being the best choice for his area.

SITE AND SOIL

Sun and shelter is what sweet corn needs in the way of climate – cold spots will produce spindly plants that never even flower. A soil well manured for a previous crop is best. It should be dug over in winter and a couple of handfuls of blood, bone and fishmeal raked into each square metre (yard) before planting or sowing. On dry soils the plants will never come to much, so make sure that they can sink their powerful roots into some moist but well-drained earth.

SEED SOWING

If you take my advice you'll sow your seeds individually in small peat pots of a peat-based potting compost in April, germinating them indoors on a windowsill. Plants raised like this *always* get away better than those sown in the open. In the north such a start is essential if the plants are to

have time to fruit. Only in very mild areas should you bother to sow outdoors; in which case sow three seeds 1cm (½in) deep at 45cm (18in) stations on the square. Sweet corn needs to be well pollinated if cobs are to form, so give it every chance of succeeding by planting it in blocks of short rows rather than one or two long ones. Outdoor sowings will get away better if covered with cloches or even jam jars. Thin the resulting seedlings to leave one at each station. Harden off indoor-raised plants before planting out.

PLANTING

Early May planting can be practised if you have cloches to spare; if you haven't then wait

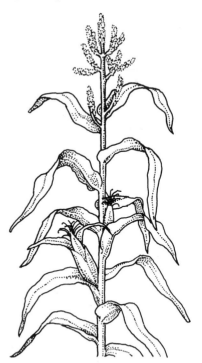

The male flowers at the top of the sweet corn plant should be tapped as soon as they open so that pollen is discharged on to the females below. You can tell when the cobs are ripe, as they start to lean further away from the stem.

until late May in the south or early June in the north. Plant once again at 45cm (18in) spacings both ways. Soak the pots and compost before you plant out, and make sure that the soil outdoors is moist. Water each plant in.

CULTIVATION

Remove any cloches in mid-June or before if the leaves touch the glass. Hoe between the plants and trap slugs if these are a nuisance (see page 133). Protect young plants from bird damage with netting. Apply plenty of water in dry weather to keep the plants growing vigorously. When the male flowers open at the top of the plants, tap them regularly to discharge pollen onto the females lower down the stem. Support the plants with canes if they look like toppling, or earth them up a little (the fat buttress roots that spring from the lower stem joints will help to support the plants). A monthly liquid feed from July to September will be beneficial.

HARVESTING

When ripe the cobs will angle themselves further away from the stem (observing this will save you from spoiling your cobs by using the old test of sticking a fingernail into a grain – when milky sap rather than clear fluid comes out the cob is ripe). The tassels wither and turn brown before the cob ripens, so there's no need to watch carefully before this time. Use the cobs as fresh as possible.

STORAGE

Corn cobs freeze well.

PESTS AND DISEASES

Frit fly may attack outdoor sowings.

SHOW TIPS

Grow as recommended. Select fresh, ripe cobs for showing. They should be well-filled with corn right to the tips and the base with no gaps. The grains should be plump, evenly coloured and in straight rows. Suitable varieties include First of All and John Innes Hybrid.

IN BRIEF

Site and soil   Plenty of sun and shelter; good, well-drained soil
Sow   April – indoors or in a greenhouse; Early May – outdoors
Plant   Early May – under cloches; late May or early June – in the open
Successional sowing   Unnecessary
Harvest   Late July if you're lucky but more likely August/September
Effort   **

TOMATO

Always dicey outdoors – particularly in the north – but even if there is a shortage of ripe fruits you can always make green tomato chutney!

VARIETIES

You can either grow single-stemmed tomatoes outdoors, or you can plump for the bush varieties which are less troublesome because they don't need stripping of their sideshoots and they won't require stakes. I prefer the bush varieties and can recommend The Amateur and Alfresco as among the best. Both grow to just over 30cm (1ft). Marmande is single-stemmed but produces those tasty lobed fruits so popular on the continent, and good old Moneymaker is still well worth growing.

SITE AND SOIL

Pick your sunniest, most sheltered spot for the tomatoes. They will be quite happy on well-cultivated ground that was manured for a previous crop. Scatter a couple of handfuls of blood, bone and fishmeal over each planting spot just before setting out the plants.

SEED SOWING

Sow the seeds indoors in mid-March in the south; in early April in the north. Sow two seeds to a peat pot of peat-based potting compost and germinate them in the airing cupboard. Take the pots out as soon as the first seedling is spotted. Keep them on a sunny windowsill and thin to leave one seedling in each pot. Keep the plants well watered and in excellent light at all times or they will become tall and spindly. Gradually harden them off until planting time – early May if they can be given cloche protection; late May (south) or early June (north) if not.

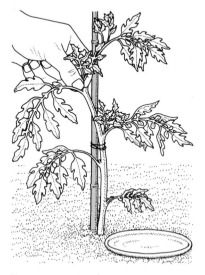

Tomatoes are much easier to water if you sink a large flowerpot into the soil alongside each one at planting time. To water, fill the pot to the brim. Pinch out the sideshoots from single-stemmed varieties, but not bush types.

PLANTING

If you don't want the bother of raising your own plants, buy them from a nursery or garden centre during May. Plant when the first flower cluster is visible. Plant with a trowel spacing the plants 45cm (18in) apart in both directions. Sink a 12cm (5in) flowerpot into the soil alongside each plant – it makes watering and feeding much easier when the soil is dry in summer (simply fill it to the brim from your can or hose). Single-stemmed varieties should be staked with a stout 1.25m (4ft) cane immediately. Loosely tie the stem to the cane with soft twine. Water each plant in.

CULTIVATION

All the sideshoots should be removed from single-stemmed varieties and their stems tied to their canes at regular intervals. Water the plants daily in summer and feed them with liquid tomato fertiliser once a fortnight as soon as the little green fruits start to swell. Spread dry straw underneath bush varieties in June so that their fruits are kept clear of the soil. Stop single-stemmed varieties when they have made four trusses of fruits – simply cut or pinch out the tip of the central shoot.

HARVESTING

Pick the fruits as soon as they have changed colour. In mid-September cloches can be stood over the plants (at this point the single-stemmed varieties can be untied from their canes and laid

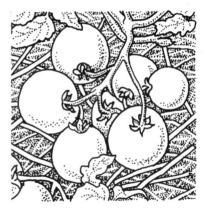

Straw spread around your bush tomatoes will keep the fruits off the ground and may encourage earlier ripening.

on a bed of straw so that cloches can be placed over the row). In mid-October clear the plants of any unripened fruit and bring it indoors.

STORAGE

Green tomatoes do not need light to ripen them – they can be put in a cupboard or drawer where warm temperatures and a concentration of ethylene gas (which they give off) will bring about their maturity. A ripe apple or banana put in with them will speed up the process.

PESTS AND DISEASES

Tomatoes have more than their fair share of problems, but you are only likely to encounter one or two of the following: whitefly, eelworm, wireworm, blossom end rot, stem rot, potato blight, leaf mould, virus diseases, blotchy ripening.

IN BRIEF

Site and soil   Sunny, very sheltered spot; rich but not freshly manured soil

Sow   Mid-March to early April indoors or in a greenhouse

Plant Early May – under cloches; late May or early June – in the open

Successional sowing   Unnecessary

Harvest   August and September

Effort   **

SHOW TIPS

It is usually the greenhouse-grown tomatoes that win prizes on the showbench – especially in wet summers when outdoor crops will not ripen in time. However, the points to look for in a good fruit are the same. It should be just ripe – not over or under. It should be of a good, rounded shape and medium sized. The calyx (the green spider on the top) should be fresh and not withered. The fruits should all be firm and of an even size and ripeness. Ensure this by picking them when they are half ripe from about a week before the show. Gather more fruits as they half-ripen and store them all indoors in a cool room. Make the final selection immediately before setting out for the show. Suitable varieties include: Herald (greenhouse growing) and Alicante (greenhouse or outdoor).

TURNIP

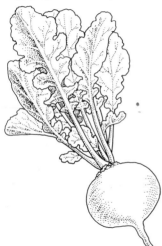

A fast-growing crop worth cultivating both for its tender roots and its tasty leaves which can provide welcome spring greens.

VARIETIES

For the early sowings under cloches use Purple Top Milan or Snowball (well named because young roots melt in the mouth). From March to May Snowball is still the best choice, but for June to September sowings go for Golden Ball which keeps well.

SITE AND SOIL

Pick an open, sunny spot and a piece of ground which was manured for a previous crop. Dig the soil well during winter, applying lime if it is acid, and then a week before sowing dust over the ground with a general fertiliser and lightly fork it into the surface. Turnips need to be grown fast (like radishes) so don't sow them on dry or very poor soil where they will never come to much. They like a firm but well-cultivated seedbed.

SEED SOWING

Sow the seeds thinly in 1cm (½in) deep drills spaced 23cm (9in) apart for the earliest crops, 30cm (1ft) apart for later crops which will produce more top growth. Thin the seedlings early so that they can instantly swell their roots. Early sowings should be thinned to 10cm (4in) and later crops to 23cm (9in). August and September sowings for spring greens need not be thinned at all.

CULTIVATION

Cloches should be put over the ground two weeks before the earliest sowing is made and removed when the crop is harvested. All crops should be watered well when necessary and a hoe pushed between the rows to cut down weeds.

HARVESTING

The best turnips are those which are rather smaller than a tennis ball, so pull the roots as soon as they are of a usable size – don't be greedy and wait for them to grow too fat or they'll be woody. Late summer sowings will stay in the ground right through winter to yield harder roots and tasty turnip tops in spring. Cut the leaves as you need them – more will sprout from the cut stump.

STORAGE
Winter crops can be left in the soil in mild areas with no more than a covering of straw. Alternatively lift the roots in October, cut off their tops and store undamaged roots in boxes of dry sand in a frostproof shed or garage.

PESTS AND DISEASES
Flea beetle is the only pest likely to attack turnips; mildew, soft rot and clubroot are the commonest diseases. The quicker your crop is grown, the less likely it is to come to any harm.

SHOW TIPS
Grow as recommended, making sure that there is no check to development. Sow in May choosing a variety such as Snowball. The roots chosen for showing should be the size of a cricket ball, clean, unblemished and tender. The taproots should be small and the leaves should be cut off 8cm (3in) above the top of the root. Trim off any fine roots.

IN BRIEF

Site and soil   Sunny site; moderately rich soil which is not prone to drought
Sow   Mid-to late February – under cloches; March to September – in the open
Successional sowing interval   3 weeks
Harvest   May onwards (all year round)
Effort   *

---

7 HERBS ON THE ALLOTMENT

A selection of some of our most popular herbs, all of which can be grown on the allotment. From top left: fennel, thyme, sage, tarragon, basil, chives, rosemary, marjoram, parsley and mint.

No self-respecting cook would be without a few herbs to enhance the flavour of meat and vegetables, soups, fish, stews and salads. Once mint was the only herb to grace the allotment, but now it's as well to have a few more growing flavours at your fingertips to satisfy discerning diners.

I've no space here to write at length about these obliging plants (see Further reading), so I'll content myself with describing in brief detail my top 10 herbs that are relatively easy to grow in any ordinary soil and with plenty of sun. Position them where they are easy to pick and where you can admire their beauty. As plot edgers they are very much at home and you won't have to muddy your boots to pick them in wet weather.

BASIL

Bushy plant growing to 30cm (1ft) or so with large green leaves.
Site and soil Sunny, sheltered spot; well-drained soil.
Plant Late June (half-hardy; killed by frost).
Cultivation Pinch shoot tips regularly and remove flowers.
Propagation Annually from seed. Sow under glass/indoors in March. Outdoors late May.
Harvest All summer. Dry some leaves before flowering.
Uses Always recommended for use with tomatoes, salads, soups and sauces with meat, game, poultry, eggs and cheese. Basil is a knockout on buttered carrots!

CHIVES

Clump-forming plant with narrow, onion-flavoured leaves. Grows to around 23cm (9in); pretty mauve flowers.

Site and soil Sunny or slightly shady spot; good soil.

Plant Spring or autumn.

Cultivation Cut tired plants to within 2.5cm (1in) of the ground in summer to encourage regeneration.

Propagation By division of clumps in spring every three years. Seeds can also be sown outdoors in April.

Harvest Fresh from spring to autumn. It does not dry successfully.

Uses Add as a garnish chopped into tiny pieces. Use on eggs, salads, in soups and wherever its delicate onion flavour is needed.

FENNEL

A whopper at around 1.5m (5ft) but the feathery leaves give the plant a graceful appearance. Aniseed flavour.

Site and soil Sunny spot; well-drained soil (likes chalk).

Plant Spring.

Cultivation Plant can be kept shorter by pinching out shoot tips. Dies down in winter.

Propagation Division of clumps in spring; seeds sown outdoors in spring.

Harvest Fresh in summer; can dry for winter use but some flavour lost.

Uses Both leaves and seeds used for flavouring. Shoots used in Provençal cooking. Used especially with fish, pork and lamb.

MARJORAM

Low, bushy herb up to 23cm (9in) high. Make sure you get the perennial kind called pot marjoram. It has pale green leaves and pinkish lilac flowers. Mild thyme flavour.

Site and soil Sunny, sheltered spot; well-drained soil.

Plant Spring.

Cultivation Clip over occasionally with garden shears when straggly. Cloche protection enjoyed in winter.

Propagation Divide or take cuttings in spring.

Harvest Fresh all summer. Dry some leaves before flowers appear, but flavour retained better if herb is frozen.

Uses In stuffings, salads and sauces; anywhere where a rich, savoury flavour is needed.

MINT

Rampant plant up to 45cm (1½ft) high. Variously scented of mint, apples, eau-de-cologne and pineapple.

Site and soil Any site; any soil except really dry stuff.

Plant Spring or autumn.

Cultivation Best grown in a large pot or in a bucket or bottomless bowl sunk into the ground – this

Mint will quickly take over your entire allotment if you let it. Restrain its eagerness by planting it in a sunken bucket, the base of which has been perforated to allow drainage.

stops it from spreading too rapidly. Pinch regularly to encourage bushiness. Cut to ground in autumn.

Propagation Divide in spring.

Harvest Fresh from spring to autumn. Dry or freeze just before flowering.

Uses With lamb in sauce or jelly; for fruit cups and with peas, soups and salads. Freeze sprigs in ice cubes.

PARSLEY

Fuzzy-leaved plant with rich green foliage. Height around 15cm (6in). Makes a good edging plant.

Site and soil Sun or light shade; good soil.

Plant Spring.

Cultivation Cut off any flower-heads. Protect with cloches or straw in winter.

Propagation Sow seeds every spring (they always come up if you sow them on Good Friday)! Germination is slow. Plant lasts only one-and-a-half years.

Harvest Right through the year (except in the heart of winter). Dries poorly; freezes well.

Uses For garnishing just about everything and for making parsley sauce. Freeze sprigs in ice cubes.

ROSEMARY

Tall evergreen shrub with narrow dark green leaves. Grows to around 1.5m (5ft) if you let it. Leaves taste sweetly savoury.

Site and soil Sunny, sheltered spot; ordinary soil.

Plant Spring.

Cultivation Pinch out shoot tips to keep a respectable size.

Propagation Take cuttings in spring; sow seeds outdoors in April/May.

Harvest Fresh all the year round. Can dry for convenience in early summer.

Uses Delicious in stuffings and as flavouring for lamb.

SAGE

Small bush with grey-green or green and yellow, pale purple, white, pink and purple leaves. (The variegated forms are prettiest and taste just as good as the ordinary sage.) Height around 30cm (1ft).

Site and soil Sunny spot; well-drained soil.

Plant Spring.

Cultivation Prune hard back in summer to encourage new shoots.

Propagation Divide in spring; take cuttings in summer.

Harvest Fresh nearly all the year round. Dry some leaves for convenience in summer. Used in stuffings for many meats and also as a flavouring for cooked vege-tables. It's a good garnish too.

TARRAGON

Upright plant growing to 60cm (2ft) or so. The leaves are narrow and pale green. Make sure you get French tarragon and not the inferior Russian.

Site and soil Very warm and sheltered; well-drained soil.

Plant Spring.

Cultivation Cover with straw or cloches in winter. Cut back to promote more shoots in spring.

Propagation Divide in spring.

Harvest Fresh in summer. Freeze for winter use.

Uses Chopped leaves used to flavour soups, sauces, vinegars and the like. Good on chicken and fish.

THYME

Aromatic carpeter 8cm (3in) with tiny dark green leaves. Strong savoury flavour.

Site and soil Sunny spot; well-drained soil.

Plant Autumn or spring.

Cultivation Cut old plants back quite hard in spring to keep them within bounds and encourage new shoots.

Propagation Divide or take cuttings in spring.

Harvest Use fresh nearly all the year round. Cut for drying before flowering.

Uses In stuffings and with meats, vegetables, soups, stews and fish. Good when chopped and scattered over salads.

STORING HERBS

Use fresh herbs whenever you can for they always have the best flavour. Dried herbs are useful in winter and should be gathered and prepared carefully so that they retain their flavour as much as possible. Pick suitable shoots and leaves in summer just before the plants flower. Place your harvest in brown paper bags and store these in a warm, dark place. When the leaves are completely dry, crush them and bottle them in airtight containers which are again stored in the dark. That way you should be able to satisfy your tastebuds well into winter.

Some herbs lose their flavour when dried but will retain it if frozen. Place sprigs of mint and parsley in the bottom of ice cube trays before filling them with water. Use the decorated cubes for fruit cups and squashes. Other herbs for freezing can simply be washed, dried and placed in polythene bags before being consigned to the freezer. They will flop when defrosted but will still retain their flavour.

8
A-Z OF FRUIT CROPS

The gardener looking for apples and pears under this heading will be disappointed. There is seldom room for trees on most allotments (even though they can be grown in restricted forms) and I am afraid there is no room for them in these pages either. I have stuck to the bush and cane fruits that yield generously and take up little room. Strawberries, too, are covered, so don't despair of having your fruit and cream in time for Wimbledon.

I have given all the cultural details necessary under each fruit, but I want here to sing the praises of that simple (but often rather expensive) piece of equipment, the fruit cage. Nearly all the soft fruits (those which grow on bushes rather than trees) are adored by birds. Bullfinches and sparrows will eat the buds in winter, and blackbirds and pigeons may eat the fruits in summer. Netting individual bushes is a fiddly and time-consuming business, so if you can afford to cover the entire portion of the allotment that is devoted to fruits, so much the better. Remove the netting at blossom time to allow pollinating insects to do their work, and make sure it is not weighed down by snow in winter. Other than this it should not give

you much bother and the nylon netting should last for years. (See page 153 for suppliers.)

Do make sure when you buy fruit trees and bushes that you are getting healthy, disease-free plants. Virus diseases in particular can cripple fruit bushes and reduce their yields tremendously. Certified stock is what you should ask for, and if this is not available (as in the case of red currants for instance) then rely on the reputation of the nursery.

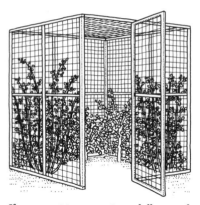

If you want to guarantee a full crop of fruit each year it's worth investing in a fruit cage, or making one yourself from timber and nylon mesh. Make sure it's totally bird proof – if birds get in and can't get out they can easily injure themselves.

BLACKBERRY & LOGANBERRY

Easy to fit into any plot, modern blackberries are high yielding and, if you choose well, tasty too. Loganberries are grown in the same way and produce tangy crimson berries in mid- to late summer.

VARIETIES
The ideal way to choose a blackberry is to sample its fruits during the summer before planting. Among the best varieties are John Innes, which is particularly sweet, and Oregon Thornless which will cut down on the injuries you receive from cruelly barbed brambles. Himalaya Giant is the beefiest of the breed so if you choose it make sure it can be given plenty of room. It is a very heavy cropper. Of the loganberries LY59 is by far the best, and its thornless variety L654 will again appeal to the sensitive. Don't buy any loganberry that is not labelled with one of these numbers – it may well be a poor fruiter.

SITE AND SOIL
Blackberries are among the most obliging of plants and will thrive equally well in sun or light shade. Loganberries prefer a sunny spot. Plant both against a fence at one end of the plot, or where they can act as screens for eyesores like compost heaps and sheds. There is no doubt that rich, moisture-retentive soil will produce the heaviest crops, but any ordinary earth which has been dug over during the autumn and enriched with well-rotted manure, compost or even peat will yield a respectable harvest. There's no need to go mad with the soil preparation: a patch 1m (3ft) square where the berry is to be planted will be quite sufficient. Make sure it is thoroughly cleared of perennial weed roots. Immediately before planting lightly fork in three handfuls of blood, bone and fishmeal over the prepared area.

SUPPORT SYSTEM
The long, arching stems or 'canes' of blackberries and loganberries would make a real nuisance of themselves if allowed to sprawl, so they are tied in to a fence-like support system. Each plant (and the average garden will need no more than one of each) will take up at least 3.75m (12ft) of fence. A 2-m (6-ft) high post and wire fence with horizontal wires at 45cm (18in) intervals is all you need. The posts should be positioned every 2m (6ft) along the fence and the wire should be of a heavy gauge. If a wooden fence already exists, then equip it with horizontal wires held in place by staples or screw eyes.

PLANTING
Plant at any time between November and March when the canes are dormant. At the foot of the support system dig a hole large enough to accommodate the roots of the plant. Trim off any damaged roots with a pair of secateurs and then space out the rest in the hole. Gradually return the soil, firming it into place with your feet, until the plant is well anchored and the soil at the same level on the stem as it was in the nursery. Cut back the stems to just above a visible bud about 23cm (9in) above ground level.

CULTIVATION AND PRUNING
In February scatter three handfuls

of a general fertiliser around the base of the plant and in late March spread a 8-cm (3-in) thick mulch of organic matter around it to keep the soil moist and suppress weed growth. As the new canes grow tie them into the wires in a fan formation, leaving a gap over the centre of the plant.

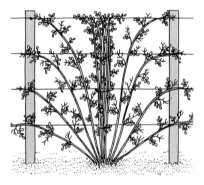

A stout post and wire fence makes a good support for blackberries and loganberries. Tie the one-year-old fruiting branches in a fan formation and take the new stems up the centre in a group as they grow.

Apply copious supplies of water in dry weather. In the second and subsequent years the new canes which arise in summer are tied together in the vacant centre portion and allowed to stretch upwards. As soon as the canes in the fan have fruited they are cut out at ground level and the new canes let down and tied in in their place. Canes fruit in their second year so no crop will be harvested in the first summer after planting. When the fruit starts to form it might be necessary to protect it from birds. Hang sheets of plastic netting in front of the plant to discourage attack.

HARVESTING
The blackberries should be picked as soon as they are black and glossy; the loganberries when they are deep crimson and tender to the touch. Pull both berries from their 'plugs' which can be left on the plant.

STORAGE
Both blackberries and loganberries can be jammed and frozen.

PESTS AND DISEASES
Exactly as for raspberries (see page 123).

PROPAGATION
Bend down a healthy shoot in July and bury its tip in the surrounding soil – holding it in place with a

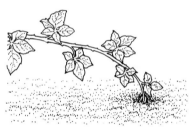

Blackberries are easy to propagate. Simply bury a stem tip in the soil; as soon as it has rooted and sent up a new shoot it can be transplanted to the site where it is to grow.

'hairpin' made from stout wire. A shoot will eventually emerge and this can be detached with its roots the following spring and planted where it is to grow. The operation is known as tip layering.

SHOW TIPS
Feed and water plants freely to keep them growing and cropping

IN BRIEF

Site and soil Sunny or slightly shady site; any reasonable soil that is not too dry; crop best on rich soil
Plant November to March
Harvest July to September
Effort **

without check. Choose large and perfectly formed fruits that are well matched. They should be cut with their stalks and should show no blemishes. The colour must be strong and the gloss high (on blackberries) to be sure of doing well.

BLACK CURRANT

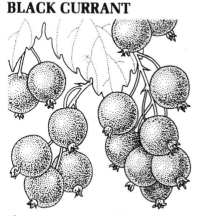

The most vigorous of the currants and the most popular. Grow black currants if you have space to spare and where they can provide shelter (but not shade) for tender vegetables.

VARIETIES
There are many to choose from but Ben Lomond is my first choice. This good all-rounder is a compact grower and so suitable for small allotments and gardens. It has a good flavour and shows a resistance to American gooseberry mildew and to frost damage. Tor Cross and Mendip Cross will mature earlier, as will the old favourite Boskoop Giant. This last variety is large and spreading so give it plenty of space. Baldwin is the latest-maturing variety and the most popular. It crops well and is reasonably compact.

SITE AND SOIL
Plant where the bushes will have room to grow in a spot that is sunny or slightly shaded. Avoid frost-pockets which can dramatically reduce yields. Acid ground should be limed in the autumn before planting. Dig over the soil in early winter working in generous supplies of well-rotted organic material – compost, manure or peat if nothing else is available. Lightly fork in a dusting of general fertiliser a few days before planting.

PLANTING
Buy two-year-old bushes which are certified free of virus diseases (these can cripple the plants and make them poor croppers). Plant the compact varieties 1.5m (5ft) apart on the square; the more vigorous varieties like Boskoop Giant will be happier at a 2m (6ft) square spacing. Trim any broken roots from each plant and dig a hole large enough to accommodate the remaining roots. Spread them out and then return the soil, firming it with your feet as you do so. When planted the bush should be about 5cm (2in) deeper than it was in the nursery (look for the old soil mark on the stem). This will encourage the stem bases to produce more roots, so establishing and anchoring the plant more thoroughly. After planting cut all the stems back to buds 5cm (2in) above soil level. If money is short buy only half the number of bushes you need and use the prunings as cuttings. They root very easily and can be pushed into the soil in groups of three on the spot where they are to grow. Make the cuttings 25cm (10in) long and leave just the top 5cm (2in) showing above ground level.

CULTIVATION AND PRUNING
Make sure that the plants do not go short of water in their first year. Remove weed growth with a hoe and mulch around the plants with organic matter in spring.

New black currant bushes should be pruned back hard after planting, but the stems removed can be used as cuttings to raise more plants. Make the cuttings 25cm (10in) long and bury all but the top 5cm (2in).

Through the first summer the plants will produce several new stems and it is these that will carry fruits in the following year. Black currants grow to between 1.25 and 2m (4 and 6ft) high and as much across. Each succeeding February scatter a dusting of general fertiliser around each plant before mulching the following month. Always water well in dry weather. Pruning is carried out each year in winter when the leaves have fallen. Cut out at ground level any spindly shoots and a few old branches so that a well-spaced framework of healthy young stems is retained. Remove no more than one third of the stems at pruning time, but do not be tempted to leave a dense thicket which will reduce cropping and make subsequent pruning a nightmare. Birds adore currants. Net the plants if necessary both in winter (to protect the buds) and in summer as soon as the fruits start to fatten.

HARVESTING
Pick the fruits as soon as they are ripe. Cut off the entire strig (small clusters of stalks which hold the berries) if they are to be kept for a few days; pick the fruits individually if they are to be used immediately. One bush will yield around 4.5kg (10lb) of fruit.

STORAGE
Blackcurrants freeze well.

PESTS AND DISEASES
Big bud mite (black currant gall mite), aphids and birds are the most likely pests; reversion virus, leaf spot, rust and American gooseberry mildew are diseases which may strike.

SHOW TIPS
Never allow the bushes to go short of water or nutrients. Mulch annually with well-rotted manure in spring and feed with blood, bone and fishmeal three times through the growing season at monthly intervals. Prune as recommended to keep the bushes vigorous. Wellington XXX and Boskoop Giant are good choices for showing. The bunches should be gathered entire and the strig left intact. Choose the fullest bunches possible so that there are no gaps where berries failed to form. The berries should be large, ripe, uniform, glossy and of a rich 'black' colour (if that's possible!). The stalks should not show any sign of shrivelling.

IN BRIEF

Site and soil Sheltered site in sun or gentle shade; avoid frost pockets. Good, rich, well-drained soil that is not too acid. Avoid very dry ground.
Plant November to March
Harvest July and August
Effort **

RED & WHITE CURRANT

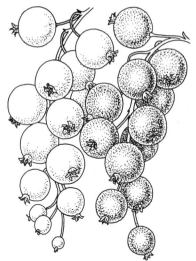

Less demanding of space than black currants but also less in demand in the kitchen. Still, they are fun to grow (and decorative too) if you have space to spare. Both red and white currants make delectable jelly and jam, mouth-watering pies and intoxicating wines.

VARIETIES
Red Lake is the most popular red currant, and deservedly so since it produces good crops of flavour-some berries mid-season. Laxton's No. 1 is rather earlier, yielding in July. Rondom is one of the later-maturing types, cropping in August. White Versailles is the white currant most often recommended and most widely grown, but White Dutch and White Grape are also well worth growing.

SITE AND SOIL
Exactly as for black currants (see page 115).

PLANTING
There is no certification scheme for red and white currants, so make sure you buy from a reputable supplier who is likely to sell healthy stock. Plants may be one or two years old and should possess at least three stems on top of a short 'leg' or trunk. Plant the

bushes to the same depth as they were planted in the nursery, leaving the leg showing above ground level. Space the plants 1.5m (5ft) apart on the square. Immediately after planting cut back all the stems to half their length. Cut to an outward-facing bud if possible to encourage the formation of a good branch structure in the first year.

Prune red and white currants much less drasticallly than the black variety after planting. The 'leg' should hold the stems clear of the ground and after planting, the stems should be shortened by half. Cut to an outward-facing bud.

CULTIVATION AND PRUNING
Scatter a dusting of general fertiliser around each plant in February, and top the soil with a thick mulch later in spring. Water each bush thoroughly in dry spells. In April or May scatter one handful of sulphate of potash around each bush to aid fruit formation. Red and white currants fruit on older wood, so try to build up a goblet-shaped bush (open in the centre) composed of six or eight main shoots. Remove one or two of the oldest stems each year, cutting them out completely in the dormant season (November to March). Allow one or two new

stems to replace them. Other than this pruning, another trimming should be carried out in July when all sideshoots should be shortened to about six leaves. Bird protection will be necessary in winter (to protect the buds) and in summer (to protect the ripening fruits).

HARVESTING
Cut the entire strigs of fruits as soon as they are ripe. One bush will yield up to 4.5kg (10lb) of fruit.

STORAGE
Freeze or preserve the fruits.

PESTS AND DISEASES
Aphids, red currant blister aphids, capsids and sawfly caterpillars can be a nuisance. Leaf spot and coral spot are the only diseases likely to be encountered.

PROPAGATION
Exactly as for gooseberries (see page 120).

SHOW TIPS
Grow as recommended and choose full bunches of fruits that are ripe, free of blemishes, glossy and of a rich colour. Size is important too. Red Lake is a good red currant for showing, and White Versailles is the best white currant.

IN BRIEF

Site and soil Sunny or slightly shady spot; good, well-drained soil
Plant November to March
Harvest July and August
Effort **

GOOSEBERRY

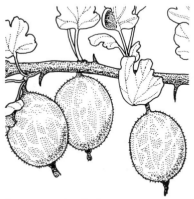

As a tangy fresh dessert or in jams and pies the gooseberry is an invaluable early-cropping fruit which should be found a place on any plot.

VARIETIES
There are two kinds of gooseberry – those grown for dessert (D) and those grown for culinary use (C). Those marked (CD) are dual purpose. Take your pick from the following (the numbers 1, 2 and 3 indicate the time of ripening – 3 being the latest – and the colours of the berries are also shown): Careless (C) (2) white; Golden Drop (D) (1) yellow; Keepsake (CD) (1) green; Lancashire Lad (CD) (2) red; Langley Gage (D) (2) yellow; Leveller (CD) (2) yellow; May Duke (CD) (1) red; Whitesmith (CD) (3) green. Many old and curiously named varieties are still available and should be tried by all those who maintain that gooseberries don't taste like they used to (see Appendix I for suppliers).

SITE AND SOIL
Select an open site if possible, though a gently shaded spot may still produce good bushes. Avoid frost pockets. Dig the soil during early autumn, working in well-rotted organic matter and removing all perennial weed roots. A week before planting scatter two handfuls of a general fertiliser

over each square metre (yard) and lightly hoe it in.

PLANTING

The bushes can be planted at any time between November and March, though the earlier the better as far as establishment goes. Trim each bush of any broken roots and suckers (shoots arising from below the original soil level). Dig a hole large enough to accommodate the roots and sit the plant in place. Gradually return the soil, firming it with your feet, until the plant sits at the level of the old soil mark on the stem. Like red and white currants, gooseberries are grown on a clean 'leg' or stem about 15cm (6in) long and this should hold the branches clear of the ground. Space the plants 1.5m (5ft) apart in both directions.

CULTIVATION AND PRUNING

If you have planted one-year-old bushes, cut all the branches back by one half after planting, making all the cuts just above a bud. Do the same with two-year-old bushes, also reducing the side-shoots by half and cutting out those which cause overcrowding. You should aim for a well-spaced framework of six or eight main

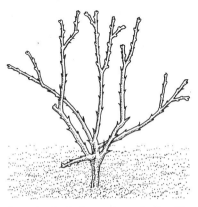

A newly planted gooseberry bush with all its stems shortened by half. Weeping varieties are cut back to upward-facing buds, and ordinary varieties to outward-facing buds.

branches. Remove any suckers that form and also any spindly shoots. Gooseberry stems are often 'weeping' in habit and although it is normally best to prune shoots back to an outward facing bud, any weeping stems should be pruned to a bud which points upwards (and therefore inwards). This will encourage a more erect habit which keeps the fruits clear of the soil and allows routine cultivation. In the first year of establishment make sure that the plants do not go short of water. Scatter one handful of sulphate of potash around each bush in February, and lay a mulch of organic matter over the surrounding soil in March every year after dusting the soil with a general fertiliser. Established bushes will need pruning twice a year: first in winter cut all the main shoots back by half, and then reduce the sideshoots to about three buds. Remove some shoots completely to keep the bush open. In early July shorten the sideshoots to about five leaves – this will encourage the production of buds that will carry next year's crop. As the bushes age, allow new branches to replace elderly ones. Through the growing season keep down weeds by hoeing (very shallowly for the roots will be near the surface), and protect the bushes from birds both in winter and as the fruits start to ripen. Thin the fruits in late May if they are closely packed – allow 5cm (2in) between adjacent berries – and use the pickings (thinnings) in a pie.

HARVESTING AND STORAGE

The main crop of fruits can be picked as soon as the berries are ripe (they will soften slightly). One bush should yield about 4.5kg (10lb) of fruit. Gooseberries preserve and freeze well.

PESTS AND DISEASES

Aphids, birds, gooseberry sawfly caterpillars and magpie moth caterpillars are the pests you might have to contend with. American gooseberry mildew is the most likely disease.

PROPAGATION

Propagation is easily effected by removing 30-cm (12-in) long shoots of firm wood in September or October. Remove the growing tip and all but the top four buds on each cutting and make a clean cut under a removed bud at the base. Insert the cuttings in a row on the vegetable plot so that the lowest bud at the top of the stem is a few centimetres above ground level. Let the cuttings root and grow freely through the following year and then lift them in autumn and treat them as one-year-old bushes.

SHOW TIPS

Spring mulching, potash feeds in spring and summer and sensible fruit thinning will produce the largest gooseberries. Careless is a good show variety. The shown fruits should be evenly matched and as large as possible. Gather them with their stalks. There are classes for both ripe and unripe berries, depending on the timing of the show. Your plateful of fruits should look fresh regardless of its state of ripeness.

IN BRIEF

Site and soil Prefers good light but a little shade tolerated; should be well-drained and moderately rich
Plant November to March
Harvest Late May and June (thinnings), July and August
Effort **

MELON

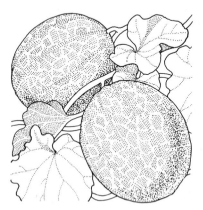

This fruit is a real treat. Until you've harvested your first melon from a home-grown plant you don't know what flavour is!

VARIETIES

Early Sweet and Sweetheart are deliciously tasty and oozing with juice. It is the canteloupe types in general that are suitable for frame and cloche growing.

SITE AND SOIL

As for cucumbers (see page 74).

SEED SOWING

As for cucumbers.

PLANTING

As for cucumbers, but train them rather differently. Pinch out the main shoot tip when six leaves have formed, then select four shoots for growing on. Train one shoot to each corner of the frame – a single plant will fill a 1.25-m (4-ft) square frame – or one to either side of a cloche-grown plant. Pinch the tips of these shoots when they have either reached the corners of the frame or grown to a length of 60cm (2ft). Pinch out any other sideshoots after three leaves.

CULTIVATION

Water and weed regularly. Spray the plants daily with tepid water if

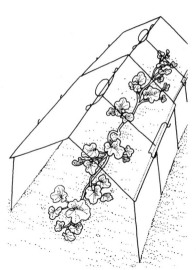

When melons are being grown under cloches, select just two main shoots and train one in either direction, pinching out all the sideshoots after three leaves have formed.

you have the time. Separate male and female flowers are produced. Ensure fruit production by pollinating four female flowers with one male at the same time so that the fruits develop simultaneously. Strip the petals off a male flower (the one with no tiny melon behind it) and push this into the centre of the four female flowers in turn. If these flowers set fruit, remove any that form afterwards. If they don't all set, remove them and repeat the pollinating operation later. Feed the plants once a week when the fruits start to swell (use liquid tomato fertiliser). Mulch the plants in late June with well-rotted manure or compost. Cut off excessive growth and remove any damaged or browned leaves as soon as they are seen. Ventilate well in sunny weather and shade the glass from mid-June onwards. As soon as the melons start to release their distinctive aroma, go easy on the water and allow the soil to dry out a little. Keep the plants too wet at this stage and the fruits will split.

HARVESTING

As soon as the fruit feels soft at the end furthest from the stalk it is ripe and can be cut and eaten. Remove and compost the plants when the fruits have been harvested.

PESTS AND DISEASES

Whitefly, red spider mites and aphids are the likely pests; stem rot is a possible disease, as is mildew.

SHOW TIPS

Grow as recommended but remove all but the most promising fruit from each plant when the fruitlets are the size of golf balls. The fruit will be judged on its ripeness (it should be neither over- nor under-ripe); its size (bearing in mind the variety); the quality of its flesh and the condition and thickness of its skin. The flesh should be thick and juicy with a good flavour and the skin should be thin.

IN BRIEF

Site and soil Sunny spot; rich, moisture-retentive soil
Sow April, indoors
Plant Late May or early June under cloches or in a frame
Harvest August and September
Effort ***

RASPBERRY

Fresh raspberries are always welcome, and if both the summer- and autumn-fruiting kinds are grown you can extend the season of harvesting well into September and October.

VARIETIES

There are plenty to choose from, but the following are, I think, among the best. They are listed in order of ripening: Malling Promise, Malling Jewel (best flavour of all), Norfolk Giant (hefty so give it strong supports), September (autumn fruiting), Zeva (autumn fruiting). Some folk would have you believe that the flavour of these late crops is not a patch on the earlies; I find that they taste delicious, even if they lack the real sweetness of Malling Jewel.

SITE AND SOIL

The summer-fruiters will put up with a bit of shade for part of the day, but they really do best in full sun. The autumn-fruiters must have all the light possible to make sure that their crop ripens before the frosts. Both types prefer a sheltered site to one which is windy. The soil must be well drained – raspberries cannot stand waterlogging. They are grown in rows and the soil should be well prepared in the autumn before planting. Dig a trench one spit deep, 30cm (1ft) wide and as long as the row and fill the bottom

with well-rotted compost, manure or even peat laced with fertiliser. Replace and firm the soil. A week before planting rake in two handfuls of blood, bone and fishmeal to each metre (yard) run of row. If you are planting several rows, make sure they run north/south so that they all get plenty of sun.

SUPPORT SYSTEM

There are as many ways of training raspberries as there are of skinning a cat, but I find that a simple post and wire fence 2m (6ft) high with horizontal wires spaced at 45cm (18in) intervals is all that is necessary. The posts can be spaced 2.5m (8ft) apart.

PLANTING

Make sure that any raspberry plants you buy are certified free of virus diseases which cripple the plants and reduce yields. Soak the canes overnight in a bucket of water before planting. Plant with a spade, taking out a hole that is wide enough to accept the roots of each cane when they are spread out. Do not plant too deeply – the roots need only be covered with 8cm (3in) of soil. Space the canes 45cm (18in) apart, re-firm the soil and immediately after planting cut them back just above a bud that is 23cm (9in) above soil level.

CULTIVATION AND PRUNING

Dust along the row with a general fertiliser in March, and then lay a mulch of well-rotted organic matter around the plants to keep in moisture and suppress weeds. As the new canes start to grow they should be gently tied into the support wires so that they are spaced about 10cm (4in) apart. Cut out the stump of old stem at ground level as soon as the new ones are doing well (do not let it flower and fruit) to ensure strength is concentrated in the new shoots. When the canes reach the topmost wire, bend them downwards and tie them in (these bent ends should be snipped off flush with the topmost wire the following

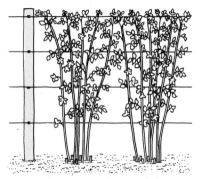
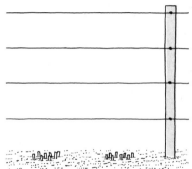

Summer-fruiting raspberries (left) and autumn-fruiting raspberries (right) are both trained on the same type of post and wire framework, but pruning is completely different. Cut out the fruiting canes of the summer-fruiting varieties as soon as the crop has been picked and tie in the new canes at an even spacing to replace them. Autumn-fruiting raspberries are pruned in February, when all the canes are cut off at ground level.

winter). Summer-fruiting raspberries will fruit on these canes in the following year, but autumn-fruiters will bear in the September after planting. Pruning of the two kinds is now quite different: every single cane of the autumn-fruiters is cut out at ground level in February. When the summer-fruiters have cropped, the fruiting canes are cut out at ground level but the new ones that grew during the summer are thinned out if necessary and tied in at 10-cm (4-in) intervals to replace them. In other words, the autumn-fruiters bear on the current season's growth and the summer-fruiters on the previous season's growth. Never let the plants go short of water, especially in the first year after planting. Hand weed among the canes and hoe lightly between the rows. Pull up any suckers that emerge too far away from the row. Net the crop as it ripens to keep off birds, and scatter two handfuls of rose fertiliser (rich in potash) along each metre (yard) run of row after harvesting and lightly hoe it in.

HARVESTING
Pick the fruits as soon as they are ripe. Pull them from their stalks leaving the 'plugs' behind. Summer-fruiters will yield up to 900g (2lb) per 30cm (foot) run of row; autumn-fruiters around 225g (½lb).

STORAGE
Raspberries freeze well.

PESTS AND DISEASES
Aphids, raspberry beetle, raspberry moth and raspberry cane midge are the likely pests; cane spot, cane blight, spur blight, botrytis and viruses are the diseases to watch out for.

PROPAGATION
Dig up and transplant suckers from healthy canes in autumn. Replace plantations after eight or

IN BRIEF

Site and soil Preferably a sunny site, but some shade is tolerated. The soil must be well drained, quite rich and not too chalky.
Plant November to March
Harvest June to July – summer fruiting; September and October – autumn-fruiting
Effort **

10 years or earlier if virus diseases disfigure the plants and reduce yields.

SHOW TIPS

Grow as recommended, being diligent about mulching and feeding. Malling Delight is a real whopper and Malling Exploit is also a good shower. The chosen fruits should be of even size (as large as possible), evenly coloured, fresh, fully ripe, unblemished and complete with stalks. Malformed fruits will not win prizes.

STRAWBERRY

They might be a bit of a fiddle to grow well, but strawberries are regarded by most gardeners as being indispensable. Grow summer-fruiting varieties for early cropping and the so-called perpetual fruiters to extend the strawberry season into October.

VARIETIES

Many gardeners will stand by the old varieties like Royal Sovereign which, for all its good flavour, is a tricky plant to grow well because it is so susceptible to virus diseases. To my palate the following are among the tastiest of the newer and more vigorous varieties. They are listed in order of ripening: Pantagruella (one of the very best), Cambridge Vigour, Redgauntlet, Tenira (delicious), Domanil. Perpetual fruiters: Aromel, Rabunda. There are lots more new varieties but I suggest you taste the fruits before you buy plants – some are rather insipid, even though the berries are bright and shiny!

SITE AND SOIL

Although they are best planted in full sun, strawberries will grow quite well in dappled shade if they have to. What they cannot stand is frost early in the season, so grow them well away from dips that act as frost pockets. Waterlogged soil will result in lack of vigour and a disease called red core (which affects the roots, not the fruits). Well-drained, well-worked soil that has been dug and manured a month before planting will suit strawberries well. Very dry soil will result in slow growth and poor crops, so the manure or compost is necessary on light land to hold on to moisture as well as to improve fertility. A week before planting scatter three handfuls of a general fertiliser over each square metre (yard) of ground and rake it into the surface. Immediately before planting, trample the soil to firm it and then rake it level again.

PLANTING

The earlier you plant, the more established the plants will become before they crop, so do try to get them in during July and August – September planting is for absent-minded gardeners. Summer-fruiting plants which cannot be set out until later in autumn or even the following spring should be relieved of the flowers they carry so that their strength is built up for the following year's crop. Perpetual fruiters can be planted as late as spring and still allowed to crop in their first year.

Always buy pot-grown plants if you can, and try to obtain those that are certified free from virus diseases. Soak the plants an hour before you are ready to set them out. Plant them with a trowel 45cm (1½ft) apart and allow 75cm (2½ft) between the rows. Plant so that the crown of the plant (the point at which the leaf stalks meet the stem) is sitting on the surface of the soil – no further above and certainly no deeper. Water the plants thoroughly immediately after they have been planted.

CULTIVATION

Give the soil a really good soak if it shows signs of drying out at any time. Hand weed between the plants and hoe between the rows. Throughout the winter remove any leaves that have turned brown and rotten. In February give the plants one good feed. Scatter some rose or tomato fertiliser (both are rich in the potash that strawberries enjoy) around the plants at the rate of one handful to two plants. Keep the fertiliser off the leaves and lightly work it into the soil with a hand fork. As soon as the fruits start to swell protect the plants from slug attack with pellets or traps (see page 133). Birds should also be kept out at this stage. Use wire netting tunnels or Westray cloches with the glass removed (these are the cloches that are fitted with black plastic netting). In early June push clean straw around the plants and under the fruits to keep them off the soil. Alternatively use bitumen strawberry mats, one to a plant, or a long sheet of black polythene which can be pierced at the required intervals and the plants drawn through. Do not mulch in this fashion too early or there is a danger that the fruits might be damaged by frost – the ground cannot radiate heat at night to warm the air above. Right through the season remove any runners (plantlets on long stems), unless you want to propagate more plants (see below). Spray the plants with

a specific aphicide if greenfly are in evidence.

HARVESTING

Pick the fruits regularly as soon as they are ripe, removing the stalk with each berry. As soon as the fruits have all been picked, cut off the foliage of all the plants and, along with the straw, burn it to kill sheltering pests and diseases. Do not be so drastic with the perpetual fruiters – just remove the older leaves and the straw.

STORAGE

Jamming is really the only way to preserve your strawberries unless you grow the new variety Totem – a summer-fruiter that reputedly freezes well.

FORCING

Strawberries growing outdoors can be brought into fruit almost a month in advance if they are covered with cloches in early February. Ventilate well at flowering time to allow insects to pollinate the blooms. Remove the cloches when the fruits have been picked and tidy up the plants. Mulch with straw or polythene as you would outdoor plants.

PESTS AND DISEASES

Aphids, slugs, birds and red spider mites are the worst pests; viruses and botrytis are the most common diseases.

PROPAGATION

Move your strawberry bed every three years to avoid the plants becoming poor and sick. During the third year allow some runners to form and in July or early August sink 8-cm (3-in) pots of potting compost into the ground around the plants, pinning a runner into each pot with a 'hairpin' of wire. Keep the compost moist and six weeks later the pots can be lifted from the soil and the runner stems cut before the new plants are set out to form a new bed. Only propagate in this way from healthy plants. If your strawberries are virus infected and poor-yielding, lift and burn them before replanting with new stock from a specialist nursery.

SHOW TIPS

Grow as recommended, choosing large fruits for showing. They should be bright and well coloured, evenly matched and at the peak of perfection with a glossy skin. The stalks should be left in place. Malformed or unevenly coloured berries should be left at home. One-year-old plants tend to produce the best show berries. Choose from the varieties mentioned above.

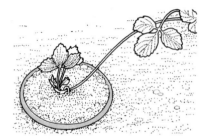

To make new strawberry plants, peg down a runner from a healthy plant into a sunken pot of compost. When the young plant is rooted and starts to grow it can be severed from its parent and planted out. Peg down your runners in July or August and you can transplant them in August or early September.

IN BRIEF

Site and soil Sunny or very slightly shaded spot which is not in a frost pocket; well-drained and well-worked soil that is moderately rich

Plant July to mid-September

Harvest May to July – summer fruiting varieties; July to October – perpetual or 'remontant' varieties

Effort ***

9 FLOWERS ON THE ALLOTMENT

The allotment might not seem to be the right place for flowers, but if you resent having to rob your borders in the garden for cut blooms, then grow a few rows of hardy annuals on the vegetable plot. They are cheap and easy to raise from seeds, can be grown in rows so that they take up little space, and when the blooms are cut the plants can be completely uprooted to make way for vegetables such as winter and spring cabbages, broccoli, kale or spinach.

SITE AND SOIL

Hardy annuals need sun so site them on a well-lit part of the plot. The ground should be well cultivated, but it need not necessarily have been dug or manured – hardy annuals do not demand rich earth and they are shallow rooting. Provided that the soil is well drained a light forking over (and a handful of general fertiliser scattered over each square metre or yard) will suit them fine. Just before sowing rake the soil to level it and break it down a little more. Do not rake it so thoroughly that it turns to dust.

WHEN TO SOW

Hardy annuals can be sown at any time between March and June when the soil is in a suitable condition. If a vegetable crop is to follow the plants then sow as early as the weather will allow.

HOW TO SOW

Sow in drills just like vegetables. Wait until the soil is moist but not so wet that it clings to your boots. Rake it level and take out a drill

Annual flowers add a splash of colour to the allotment. From top left: Calendula, Lavatera, Larkspur, Malope, Clarkia, Cornflower, Clary, Chrysanthemum, Agrostemma Milas, Acroclinium, Nigella and Dimorphotheca.

Hardy annuals for cutting

Name	Description	Height	Thin to
Acroclinium	Pink or white papery 'everlasting' flowers (correctly known as Helipterum)	45cm (1½ft)	23cm (9in)
Agrostemma Milas (corncockle)	Wide-faced flowers of lilac pink centred with white and lined with deep purple	60–100cm (2–3ft)	23cm (9in)
Calendula (pot marigold)	Double orange or yellow 'daisies'	45cm (1½ft)	23cm (9in)
Calliopsis (annual coreopsis)	Large-petalled single daises of yellow sometimes marked with orange	30–60cm (1–2ft)	15–23cm (6–9in)
Chrysanthemum (annual type)	Single daisy flowers in mixtures of white, red, orange, yellow and mahogany	45–60cm (1½–2ft)	23–30cm (9–12in)
Clarkia	Tall stems of pink, white or mauve rosettes (double varieties are best)	60cm (2ft)	23cm (9in)
Cornflower (annual)	Double blue, pink or mauve cornflowers	45–75cm (1½–2½ft)	23–30cm (9–12in)
Dimorphotheca (star of the Veldt)	White, yellow or orange daisies	23–30cm (9–12in)	10–15cm (4–6in)
Lavatera Silver Cup	Large pink trumpets on bushy plants	50–100cm (2–3ft)	30cm (1ft)
Larkspur	Blue, white or pink 'delphiniums' on slender stems	45–100cm (1½–3ft)	23–30cm (9–12in)
Malope	Loose trumpets of crimson, pink or white	75cm (2½ft)	30cm (1ft)
Nigella (love-in-a-mist)	Double pink, blue or white flowers held over fluffy leaves	30–45cm (1–1½ft)	15cm (6in)
Salvia horminum (Clary)	Tall spires of purple, pink or white leaf-like bracts	45cm (1½ft)	15cm (6in)

using a hoe held against a taut garden line. All the varieties of annual mentioned below should be sown thinly in drills 1cm (½in) deep. After sowing, mark and label the row, remove the line and rake the soil back to cover the seeds. Turn a sprinkler on the soil if it shows any sign of drying out before germination and in the weeks immediately afterwards when the young plants are growing.

CULTIVATION

As soon as the young plants are over 2.5cm (1in) high, thin them out to a spacing equivalent of half their ultimate height. Do this in stages if you like so that any seed-lings eaten by slugs can be replaced by a neighbour. The taller plants may need staking and for this you can use either twiggy pea sticks or garden canes linked with string to form an enclosure. Continue to water in dry spells and weed between the rows with a hoe.

CUTTING

Cut the blooms just as they are about to open or, with tall-stemmed blooms composed of many smaller flowers, when the lower flowers have opened. Try to cut your blooms in the early morning or evening when they are less likely to wilt. Take a bucket of water with you and stand the stems in it as soon as they are cut. If a plant can be stripped of all its blooms in one go, then pull it up and compost it. Cut the blooms with more stem than you think you will need – the excess can always be cut off later.

SWEET PEAS

These glorious flowers deserve a piece to themselves. They are favourites with allotment holders for they produce an abundance of fragrant flowers if given a spot in full sun on specially prepared soil. Here they differ from their hardy annual bedfellows, for they do best on well-manured earth prepared exactly as for runner beans (see page 53). A support system should be rigged up for the climbing shoots. Use wigwams of 2-m (6-ft) canes or a double row of sloping canes as advised for runner beans. Alternatively stretch some plastic mesh between vertical posts spaced at 2-m (6-ft) intervals and train the plants up this.

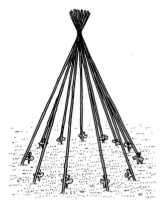

You can grow your sweet peas on the same kind of support system recommended for runner beans on page 53, but these wigwams are a better choice where space is limited or if you want to grow the plants in a flower border.

Seeds can be sown outdoors in March, April or May 2.5cm (1in) deep at the foot of the support system. Sow the seeds in pairs at 30-cm (1-ft) intervals along the row. Thin to leave the strongest seedling at each station after germination. Pinch the young plants when they are 10cm (4in) high and loosely tie in the stems as they grow. Remove any tendrils (if you have the time) and apply a liquid feed to the plants once a month. Never let the soil dry out at any time (mulch it with compost or manure in April). Cut the blooms with as much stem as possible as soon as they start to colour up.

RECOMMENDED VARIETIES

(All chosen for their scent).

Blue Noel Sutton, Evensong
Lavender Southampton, Leamington
Red Red Ensign, Blaze
White Royal Wedding, Diamond Wedding
Cream Cream Ruffles, Cream Southbourne
Purple Royalist
Mauve The Doctor, Eclipse
Rich Pink Frances Perry, Elisabeth Collins
Maroon Royalist, Black Prince

SPRING BEDDING

Wallflowers and forget-me-nots, those two stalwarts of the spring bedding scheme, are easy to raise on the allotment if space is short in the garden. Sow both in May or June on well-cultivated land. Do not sow wallflowers on ground that has grown brassicas recently (or where the brassicas will be set out later) for wallflowers also suffer from clubroot and may perpetuate the disease. Sow both flower seeds in drills 1cm (½in) deep and sow thinly to allow for subsequent growth. In July the plants should be dug up and transplanted 15cm (6in) apart in rows 30cm (1ft) apart. Transplant them to the garden in October. Never let the soil around the plants dry out (especially after they have been moved) and keep down weeds by hoeing regularly.

10 PESTS, DISEASES AND DISORDERS

Every book of this nature has to come clean and tell you what can go wrong in the garden. Sometimes your crops will not do well and then you'll need to know just how to put matters right.

Start off by giving your plants every chance to succeed. Healthy plants with adequate supplies of water, nutrients, light and air will be vigorous enough to survive many attacks by pests and diseases; the plants that are weak and struggling may well succumb instantly when faced with yet another obstacle.

Seeds and plants bought from reputable suppliers will almost always be healthy. Make sure of the cleanliness of fruit bushes by buying from a supplier who sells stock that is certified free from virus diseases (see page 152). When you are sowing seeds, try to choose varieties that are resistant to particular diseases. Catalogues should give helpful advice on this. When you are propagating your own plants, make sure that the parents are healthy and vigorous.

Above all, give the plants good growing conditions. Keep down weeds which will compete for light, nutrients and air, and which will harbour pests and diseases that can leap upon your cultivated crops.

Don't grow the same vegetable crops on the same patch of soil every year – that's just asking for trouble. Move the plants from one spot to another every season so that the soil is not exhausted of particular nutrients and specific pests and diseases do not build up their strength.

When you do spot an outbreak of a pest or disease, act quickly to stop it from spreading. First identify it, then check what damage it will do, and finally stamp it out with the right cultural technique or chemical application. Don't instantly reach for the bottle of poison – first ask yourself why the problem has occurred. If you can find a cultural error you might be able to stop the disaster from recurring. If it has come about as a result of nothing more than bad luck, take the necessary action and be philosophical!

When you have to apply a chemical, make sure you know which one to use. Insect pests can be controlled with a range of insecticides; mites with acaricides and slugs with baits or molluscicides. Larger animals such as pigeons, rabbits and mice are usually deterred rather than killed, and some form of netting which will exclude them is the best solution. Different insecticides vary in their effectiveness at controlling different insects so I have recommended particular products in the table that follows. Wherever possible try to use a specific insecticide that will kill only the pest and not other beneficial insects along with it.

Diseases of plants are usually either fungi or bacteria and cannot be controlled by spraying with insecticides. Special fungicides are recommended where necessary. Virus diseases cannot be controlled and all infected plants (which become feeble and poor-yielding) should be burned. Aphids (greenfly and blackfly) spread viruses so control the pest to prevent the disease.

Disorders have nothing to do with either pests or diseases, but they have quite a lot to do with you. They occur as a result of unfavourable growing conditions and cultural mistakes. Do a Sherlock Holmes analysis to discover what's wrong, and then take the appropriate remedial action.

Finally here are a few safety precautions to make your life (and the lives of legitimate garden creatures) safer.

1 Store all chemicals in clearly labelled containers out of the reach of pets and children.

2 Read the manufacturer's instructions and follow them carefully. Apply chemicals at the recommended times, at the recommended rates and at the recommended intervals. *Never* add one for the pot – chemists have spent years working out the correct dosage, so don't assume that a spoonful more will do a better job; it will probably kill the plant as well as the pest.

3 Wear rubber gloves when handling chemicals and wash thoroughly afterwards.

4 Allow the recommended time to elapse between spraying and harvesting.

PESTS AND DISEASES OF VEGETABLE CROPS

LEAVES, STEMS AND SHOOTS

Symptoms	Crops attacked
Shoots infested with small green, black or pinkish insects which suck sap and secrete a sticky honeydew. They also transmit virus diseases.	Wide range
Undersides of leaves infested with small white flies that fly around in circles when disturbed. Honeydew is secreted.	Wide range (including cabbages)
Leaves spotted with minute silvery dots which eventually join to form bleached areas. Fine webbing might be visible; minute pinprick sized greenish mites observed on undersides of leaves.	Cucumber, capsicums, aubergines, melons, French beans and occasionally others
Leaves eaten; silvery trails observed.	Wide range
Leaves and shoots eaten; upper part of shoots may be brown if lower stem also eaten or girdled. Black and yellow beetles or dark grey grubs visible.	Asparagus

5 Always spray in the evening when there is no wind, when few bees are about, and when the sun is not bright.

6 Avoid mixing more solution than you will need. Dispose of any surplus mixture by flushing it down the lavatory. Dispose of empty containers by capping them tightly and putting them in the dustbin.

7 Do not leave spray mixtures in sprayers after the job has been done – they will lose their effectiveness and may become toxic to plants.

8 Keep everybody out of the way while you spray, and make sure you are using the right product for the job.

HOW TO USE THE TABLE
If you can identify the pest or disease attacking your crop, look down column three until you locate it and then check in column four to see what remedial action should be taken. If you cannot identify the problem, look down the first column of symptoms and check that these apply to your crop (column two). The problem and remedy can then be found alongside.

Problem	Cure
Aphids (greenfly and blackfly)	Spray with ICI Rapid Greenfly Killer or Abol-G, neither of which is harmful to ladybirds or bees.
Whitefly	Spray with Bio Flydown or ICI Picket.
Red spider mites	Spray with any systemic insecticide or one containing Malathion or Fenitrothion. Vary the chemical used to prevent the pest building up a resistance.
Slugs or snails	Lay slug pellets under propped up flowerpots. Sink yoghurt pots into the ground around susceptible crops; fill them with beer and empty them of the bodies every morning. This method is safer where pets and wild animals are at large.
Asparagus beetle	Spray with ICI Sybol 2 or an insecticide containing Malathion.

Symptoms	Crops attacked
Foliage eaten; long, brown, pincer-tailed insects observed.	Asparagus and occasionally other crops
Edges of leaves eaten in a scalloped pattern.	Peas and broad beans
Leaves distorted, discoloured and weak.	Carrot
Leaves of seedlings spotted and holed.	Small range but especially turnips and radishes
Leaves eaten; long, greenish or green and black grubs found.	Mainly brassicas (cabbages, Brussels sprouts, broccoli, cauliflowers etc)
Leaves ripped and shredded; often only midrib left.	Brassicas
Leaves tunnelled, showing whitish ribbon markings and blisters.	Celery, celeriac, parsnip
Leaves and stems eaten and plant severely cut back. Large, round droppings or cloven hoofprints visible on soil.	Wide range
Leaves eaten; plant looks twisted, tattered and straw-coloured.	Sweet corn
Leaves distorted, twisted and bloated; bulbs soft.	Onions and occasionally leeks
Lower leaves brown and shrivelled; plants pale and stunted; tiny cysts visible on lifted roots. Crops poor.	Potato
Plants stunted, purplish and wilting – minute cysts present on roots **OR** lower leaves yellow and wilting; roots have galls (swollen lumps).	Tomato

Problem	Cure
Earwigs	Trap in flowerpots inverted on top of canes and stuffed with newspaper. Empty traps every morning into a bucket of water. Dust plants in evening with Murphy Sevin Dust.
Pea and bean weevil	Ignore mild attacks. Spray severe outbreaks with Murphy Fentro, pbi Fenitrothion or dust with ICI Sybol 2 Dust.
Carrot willow aphid	Spray with pbi Fenitrothion or Murphy Fentro.
Flea beetle	Dust with Derris as soon as seen.
Caterpillars	Pick off small infestations; spray larger outbreaks with Bio Flydown, ICI Picket or May & Baker Caterpillar Killer.
Pigeons	Erect pigeon netting over crop. Scarers seldom effective.
Celery fly	Pick off and destroy badly infected leaves; spray with a systemic insecticide or May & Baker Caterpillar Killer.
Rabbits and deer	Only effective control (apart from the gun!) is to surround area with 1.25-m (4-ft) wire fence sunk 45cm (18in) into ground at base. Chemical deterrents such as Renardine may help to repel deer which can clear fences.
Frit fly	Raise plants under glass and plant out in early June to avoid attacks. Dust with Murphy Gamma-BHC Dust as preventive measure on outdoor-sown crops.
Eelworm	Destroy infected plants; practise crop rotation; keep onions, leeks, parsnips, carrots and beans off the site for three years.
Potato cyst eelworm	Prevent by growing resistant varieties like Maris Piper and Pentland Javelin. Practise crop rotation. Destroy infected plants. Keep potatoes and tomatoes off infected ground for eight years.
Eelworm	Pull up and burn; practise crop rotation. Keep potatoes and tomatoes off infected ground for eight years.

Symptoms	Crops attacked
Stem rotten at ground level.	Cucumber, tomato, melon
Leaves mottled with yellow; plant stunted and weak; leaves puckered.	Marrow, courgette, cucumber
Leaves weakened and covered with white powder.	Cucumber, turnip, melon and brassicas
Leaves spotted and blotched with brown; whole plant may turn black and die in severe outbreak.	Broad beans
Leaves possess brown blotches that are spotted with black.	Celery and celeriac
Leaves spotted with orange.	Leeks and occasionally onions
Tissue turns soft and brown; grey fur appears.	Wide range
Bases of stems turn brown and plants keel over.	Seedlings in general
Tips of leaves turn brown and rot. Leaves turn inwards and show white mould on undersides.	Potatoes and tomatoes
Leaves curled inwards or mottled with yellow.	Potato
Leaves yellow on upper surface, purplish below. Leaves eventually turn brown and rot.	Spinach
Leaves yellowish above, purplish and mouldy below.	Tomato

Problem	Cure
Stem rot	Avoid by not planting too deeply and by dusting young plants with Murphy Bordeaux Powder. Destroy infected plants.
Mosaic virus	Prevent attacks by keeping down weeds which can act as hosts. Control greenfly which spread the disease. Destroy infected plants.
Powdery mildew	Tolerate mild attacks; spray severe outbreaks with pbi Benlate. Space plants well to prevent attacks.
Chocolate spot	Avoid by not applying too much nitrogenous fertiliser. Burn crop remains at end of season to destroy spores. Spray with pbi Benlate, ICI General Garden Fungicide or Synchemicals Bordeaux Mixture.
Leaf spot	Obtain seeds treated against the disease. Spray with pbi Dithane 945, pbi Benlate or Synchemicals Bordeaux Mixture.
Leek rust	Destroy infected foliage. Prevent by not applying too much nitrogen and by rotating crops. Clean parts edible.
Grey mould (botrytis)	Pick off infected areas if possible. Make sure soil is not deficient in potash. Prevent by spacing crops to allow air circulation and by spraying with pbi Benlate.
Damping off	Do not sow too thickly; water young plants with Cheshunt Compound if the disease has previously been a problem.
Potato blight	Destroy infected tomato plants. Prevent by growing resistant potato varieties (e.g. Maris Peer, Pentland Crown). Spray with pbi Dithane or Synchemicals Bordeaux Mixture fortnightly from July onwards in humid weather.
Virus disease	Prevent by buying certified seed potatoes and by controlling aphids which spread viruses. Destroy infected plants.
Downy mildew	Remove and destroy infected leaves. Spray plants with pbi Dithane 945. Avoid applying too much nitrogenous fertiliser.
Leaf mould	Grow resistant varieties; remove lower leaves that show signs of attack and spray plants with pbi Benlate.

Symptoms	Crops attacked
ROOTS	
Large lumps of tissue missing; holes bored so large that tap roots and tubers almost hollow.	Wide range
Leaves turn blue and plants wilt; roots eaten by maggots.	Brassicas
Leaves wilt in sun; roots tunnelled.	Carrot, parsnip
Roots possessing galls or minute cysts.	Tomato, potato
Leaves wilt and turn yellowish; bulbs eaten by white grubs.	Onion
Narrow tunnels eaten in roots.	Potato, tomato
Roots infested with purple-felted mould.	Asparagus and carrots
Upper areas of roots light brown and rotten.	Parsnip
Tubers covered with brown scabs.	Potato
Black warts appear on tubers of old varieties.	Potato
Tubers blotched with grey on outside; marked with reddish brown within.	Potato
Buds and plant centre brown and rotten.	Rhubarb
Plant dies. White fungus and black 'bootlaces' found in soil.	Rhubarb

Problem	Cure
Slugs	Avoid over-manuring. Keep surrounding area free of rubbish and crop debris. Lift crops as soon as mature – store in shed rather than soil. Cultivate soil frequently to expose slugs to birds.
Cabbage root fly	Dust soil with Murphy Soil Pest Killer or Fison's Combat Soil Insecticide.
Carrot fly	Avoid by not thinning; scatter Murphy Soil Pest Killer or Fison's Combat Soil Insecticide along drills at sowing time.
Eelworm	(See under Leaves, stems and shoots.)
Onion fly	Prevent by rotating crops. Apply Murphy Soil Pest Killer or Fison's Combat Soil Insecticide to ground at sowing time. Sets less susceptible.
Wireworm	Harvest potatoes as soon as possible when ready. Rake pbi Bromophos into ground not previously cultivated.
Violet root rot	Destroy all infected plants; do not replant these two crops on infected land for five years. Practise crop rotation.
Parsnip canker	Prevent by sowing resistant varieties, rotating crops and avoiding dryness at roots.
Potato scab	Prevent by growing resistant varieties and by not over-liming land. Affected tubers still edible.
Wart disease	Burn all infected tubers. Ministry of Agriculture must be informed. Prevent by growing new varieties which are immune.
Potato blight	(See under Leaves, stems and shoots.)
Crown rot	Dig up and burn infected plants. Prevent by ensuring good drainage. Do not replant rhubarb on infected land.
Honey fungus	Dig up and burn. Do not plant rhubarb where previously trees and shrubs grew. Do not replant rhubarb on infected soil.

Symptoms	Crops attacked
Roots brown in the centre.	Swede
Plants stunted. Roots found to be swollen and when cut open reveal holes or grubs.	Brassicas (cabbages etc)
Plants stunted and wilting; roots swollen and foul smelling. No holes or grubs present.	Brassicas
Centre of plant turns brown and rotten.	Turnip, celery

FRUITS, PODS AND SEEDS

Pods ripped and contents eaten.	Peas
Maggots found to be eating crop when pods opened.	Peas
Few seedlings emerge from soil.	Peas
Pods spotted and blotched silver grey.	Peas
Base of fruits black and sunken.	Tomato
Fruits ripen very unevenly with green, orange and red blotching.	Tomato
Fruits mottled with red and eventually black. Leaf tips brown and rotten.	Tomato
Buds unusually fat and swollen; spherical rather than pointed.	Blackcurrant

Problem	Cure
Brown heart	Due to boron deficiency. Prevent by applying a fertiliser before sowing. If disorder occurs, treat land with 30g (1oz) borax to 20 sq m (yards) and mix with sand to aid distribution.
Gall weevil	Prevent by growing in good soil so plants can withstand attacks. Dust around young plants with pbi Bromophos or ICI Sybol 2 at planting time.
Clubroot	Prevent by rotating crops. Ensure good drainage; lime acid soils. Keep down weeds. Dip roots of young plants in Murphy Systemic Clubroot Dip.
Soft rot	Prevent by rotating crops and avoiding mechanical damage. Keep down slugs which can allow disease in. Destroy infected plants. Avoid over-manuring and badly drained soils.
Sparrows	Net the crop. Deterrents seldom effective.
Pea moth	Prevent by spraying in evening one week after flowers have opened with Murphy Fentro or pbi Fenitrothion.
Mice (and occasionally fungus diseases if sown too early in wet soil)	Set traps under propped-up slates. Dress seeds with a fungicidal seed dressing to prevent disease.
Pea thrips	Spray as soon as seen with Murphy Fentro or pbi Fenitrothion.
Blossom end rot	Pick off and discard affected fruits. Prevent by ensuring that soil around roots does not dry out.
Blotchy ripening	Prevent by ensuring good supplies of food and water. Shade from scorching sun.
Potato blight	(See under Leaves, stems and shoots.)
Big bud mite	Cut out and burn infected stems in winter. Destroy badly infected bushes. Prevent by spraying with pbi Benlate as flowers open. The mite carries reversion virus. (This crippling virus infection attacks plants causing dramatic reductions in yield.)

Symptoms	Crops attacked
Shoots infested with small green, reddish or black insects sucking sap and secreting honeydew.	Wide range
Upper leaves twisted and blistered, sometimes tinged with red.	Currants and gooseberries
Leaves punctured by brown-edged holes. Some puckering.	Currants
Leaves eaten – only veins left behind.	Currants and gooseberries
Stems split and found to harbour pink maggots.	Raspberry
Leaves pale and bleached; minute mites visible; webs spun in severe attacks.	Strawberries
Flowers pinkish-purple; foliage distorted – leaves have fewer lobes. Cropping reduced.	Blackcurrant
Leaves develop small brown spots which eventually join together.	Currants
Brown spots on undersides of leaves which turn brown and fall early in season.	Currants
Leaves covered in white powdery or felted growth which eventually turns brown. Fruits also affected.	Currants and gooseberries
Stems die and are covered with raised orange spots.	Currants
Purple spots on stems; leaves and fruits also spotted. Canes develop larger grey areas.	Raspberries
Leaves wither; dark marks on canes just above soil level; canes brittle and snap easily.	Raspberries
Stem around buds turns purple then grey. Buds die and fail to grow in spring.	Raspberries
Fruits covered with greyish downy mould.	Raspberries, strawberries
Leaves distorted and mottled with yellow; plants lacking in vigour and rather stunted.	Raspberries and strawberries in particular

Problem	Cure
Aphids (greenfly and blackfly)	Spray with ICI Rapid Greenfly Killer or Abol-G.
Currant blister aphid	Spray bushes with a tar oil wash in January to kill overwintering eggs. Spray with a systemic insecticide during summer.
Capsid bug	Spray with a systemic insecticide once the petals have fallen from the flowers.
Sawfly caterpillars	Spray with pbi Fenitrothion or Murphy Fentro. If fruits are near maturity spray with Derris.
Cane midge	Dust attacked areas with Murphy Gamma-BHC dust.
Red spider mite	Spray with systemic insecticide.
Reversion virus (see above under big bud mite)	Dig up and burn infected bushes. Plant on a fresh site. Control big bud mite.
Leaf spot	Gather up and burn fallen leaves in autumn. Spray with pbi Benlate.
Rust	Gather and burn infected leaves. Spray with a copper fungicide.
American goose-berry mildew	Prevent by avoiding too rich a soil and over-crowding of stems. Destroy badly infected shoots. Spray with pbi Benlate.
Coral spot	Cut out all infected wood and paint wounds with May & Baker Seal and Heal Pruning Paint.
Cane spot	Cut out and burn infected canes. Spray with pbi Benlate as a preventative in spring.
Cane blight	Cut out completely any infected canes. Spray newly emerging canes with a copper fungicide.
Spur blight	Cut out and burn infected canes. Spray with pbi Benlate.
Botrytis	Pick off infected fruits. Spray with pbi Benlate.
Virus diseases	Dig up and burn infected plants. Keep down aphids and other pests which spread the diseases.

Symptoms	Crops attacked
Shoots wilted and dying; stems found to contain caterpillars.	Raspberry
Fruits nibbled and holed or completely missing.	Raspberries, strawberries, currants
Fruits eaten by maggots which are still visible.	Raspberries

Problem	Cure
Raspberry moth	Remove and burn infected shoots. Spray in winter with a tar oil wash.
Birds or slugs	Fruit cages or plastic netting will keep out birds. For slug control see under vegetable section.
Raspberry beetle	Spray with Derris as soon as fruits turn pink.

11 VEGETABLE FACTS AND FIGURES

STORAGE OF VEGETABLE SEEDS

Although the seedsmen would prefer gardeners to buy new seeds every year, it is possible to keep and use surplus seeds for several years provided they are stored carefully. Put the packets in an airtight container and store this in a cool, dry, dark place. The following table gives some idea of how long the different types of vegetable seed will last (still giving a high germination rate) under ideal conditions.

Some gardeners save seeds from their runner beans (and other peas and beans) each year, allowing a few pods to dry on the plant. Healthy, high-cropping plants can be grown from such seeds the following year provided that the plants from which they were culled were not F_1 hybrids. Such varieties will not produce uniform offspring and seed should never be saved from them. Consult a seed catalogue if you are in any doubt – F_1 hybrids are always marked as such. They are vigorous 'first-generation crosses' which are produced afresh each year by the seedsman – two parent plants will be cross-fertilised to produce seeds which yield vigorous and uniform plants. The seeds will be expensive but the plants are usually of extremely high quality. However, when these plants themselves are cross-fertilised, all the characteristics of their parents are redistributed unevenly through their offspring, so making for a poor crop.

Storage of vegetable seeds

Vegetable	Years	Vegetable	Years
Aubergine	5	Leek	3
Beans	3	Lettuce	4–5
Beetroot	4	Marrow/Courgette	5–6
Leaf beet	4	Melon	5
Broccoli	5	Onion	1–2
Brussels sprouts	5	Parsley	1–3
Cabbage	4–5	Parsnip	1–2
Carrot	3–4	Pea	3
Cauliflower	4–5	Pepper	4
Celeriac	5	Pumpkin	4
Celery	5–6	Radish	5
Chicory	5	Salsify	2
Corn salad	5	Scorzonera	2
Cucumber	5–6	Spinach	5
Endive	5	Sweet corn	1–2
Kale	5	Tomato	4
Kohlrabi	5	Turnip	4

Expected yields of vegetables (Approximate only)

Crop	Yield per plant	Yield per 30 cm (ft) of row
Artichoke, Globe	10–15 heads	—
Artichoke, Jerusalem	2.25–4.5kg (5–10lb)	—
Broad bean	—	225g ($\frac{1}{2}$lb)
French bean	—	110g ($\frac{1}{4}$lb)
Runner bean	—	2.25kg (5lb)
Beetroot	—	450g (1lb)
Broccoli	—	560g (1$\frac{1}{4}$lb)
Brussels sprout	—	450g (1lb)
Cabbage (spring)	—	340g ($\frac{3}{4}$lb)
Cabbage (summer/winter)	—	675g (1$\frac{1}{2}$lb)
Carrot	—	450g (1lb)
Cauliflower	—	450g (1lb)
Celeriac	—	110g (4oz)
Celery (traditional)	—	450g (1lb)
Courgette	10–20 fruits	—
Kale	—	675g (1$\frac{1}{2}$lb)
Kohlrabi	—	170g (6oz)
Leek	—	450g (1lb)
Lettuce	—	1–2 plants
Marrow	3 or 4 fruits	—
Onion	—	340g ($\frac{3}{4}$lb)
Parsnip	—	340g ($\frac{3}{4}$lb)
Pea	—	170g (6oz)
Potato (early)	—	340g ($\frac{3}{4}$lb)
Potato (maincrop)	—	675g (1$\frac{1}{2}$lb)
Radish	—	85g (3oz)
Salsify/scorzonera	—	85g (3oz)
Spinach (summer)	—	225g (8oz)
Swede	—	1.8kg (4lb)
Sweet corn	2 cobs	—
Tomato (outdoor)	1.8kg (4lb)	—
Turnip	—	285g (10oz)

VEGETABLE GARDEN CALENDAR

The calendar on the following pages is intended to provide an at-a-glance guide to the sowings and plantings taking place on the vegetable plot and the crops to be harvested at any time of year. It is intended to offer rough guidelines – don't worry if you are a few days late with anything. Above all, be guided by the weather rather than sticking slavishly to my recommendations. If the soil is cold and unworkable, wait! Seeds put into warm ground a little later than normal will soon romp away. Those buried in an icy grave may never emerge.

Crop	Jan	Feb	Mar	Apr	May	Jun	Jul	Aug	Sep	Oct	Nov	Dec
Globe artichoke				⌐•		◁						
Jerusalem artichoke		⌐ ⌐	⌐	⌐							⌐ ⌐	
Asparagus			△△	⌐••	◁							
Aubergine	△△△			⌐••		◁				••	•••	•••
Broad bean	△△△ •	•	⌐•••	⌐•••	⌐•••	••	•	•				
French bean			△△△△	⌐	•	••	•••	•••				
Runner bean			△△△△	⌐••	⌐•	••						
Beetroot		△△△ •	•	•	•	•	•	•				
Leaf beet				⌐•	•	•	•			◁		
Broccoli	△△△△	•	•	⌐•	⌐•	⌐•	•	⌐	⌐			
Brussels sprout	△△△△	△△△△	△△△△	⌐	⌐	⌐	⌐	⌐	⌐	⌐		
Cabbage — spring		△△△△	•	⌐	⌐	⌐	⌐					
— early summer			•	⌐	⌐	⌐	⌐					
— summer			•	•	⌐•	⌐•	⌐					
— savoys			•	•	•	⌐•	⌐					
— winter			•	•	•	⌐•	⌐					
Calabrese				•	•	•	•	•				
Capsicum	△△		◁		◁	◁						
Carrot			△△△△	⌐••	•	•	•					
Cauliflower — summer	△△△ •		⌐••	⌐••		◁	•		•	◁◁		
— autumn & winter				•		⌐	⌐					
Celeriac		△△△△	△△△△									
Celery		△△△△	△△△△		◁	◁	◁					
Chicory						•	•					
Corn salad				•	◁	•			•			
Cucumber			•••	△△△				••	••		◁	
Endive			•	△	•	•	•	•				
Garlic			•	△								

Kohlrabi
Land cress
Leek
Lettuce
Marrow & Courgette
Onion — spring
— maincrop
— Japanese
— autumn sown
— overwintering sets
Parsnip
Pea
Potato — early
— maincrop
Pumpkin
Radish — spring to autumn
— winter radish
Rhubarb
Salsify
Scorzonera
Shallots
Spinach — summer
— winter
— perpetual
Swede
Sweet corn
Tomato
Turnip

Key   . sow in the open   ⊱ plant in the open   ⋀ sow under cloches   ⋀ plant under cloches   ▨ harvest

149

Vegetables in season

Vegetable	J	F	M	A	M	J	J	A	S	O	N	D
Globe artichoke							─	─	─			
Jerusalem artichoke	─	─	─								─	─
Asparagus					─							
Aubergine	--	--	--							--	--	--
Broad bean	--	--	--			─	─	─		--	--	--
French bean	--	--	--			─	─	─		--	--	--
Runner bean	--	--	--		─		─	─	─	--	--	--
Beetroot	••	••	••	•			─	─	─	─	••	••
Leaf beet	─	─	─	─	─	─	─	─	─	─	─	─
Broccoli & Calabrese	--	─	─	─	─		--	--		--	--	--
Brussels sprout	─	─	─				─	--	--	─	─	─
Cabbage – spring				─	─							
Cabbage – early summer & summer					─	─	─	─	─			
Cabbage – savoys & winter	─	─	─						─	─	─	─
Capsicum	--	--	--							--	--	--
Carrot	••	••	••	•	--	--	--	─	─	─	••	••
Cauliflower	─	─	─	─	─	─	─	─	─	─	─	─
Celeriac	••	••	••	••					─	─	••	••
Celery	─	─	--	--		─	─	─	─	─	─	─
Chicory	─	─	─	─						─	─	─
Corn salad	─	─	─	─	─	─	─	─	─	─	─	─
Cucumber						─	─	─	─			
Endive	─	─	─					─	─	─	─	─
Kale	─	─	─	─							─	─
Kohlrabi							─	─	─	─	─	─
Land cress	─	─	─			─	─	─	─	─	─	─
Leek	─	─	─	─	--	--	--	--	--	─	─	─
Lettuce				─	─	─	─	─	─	─	─	─
Marrow/Courgette	••	••					─	─	─	•	••	••
Onion	••	••	••	••	••		─	─	─	•	••	••
Parsnip	─	─	─						─	─	─	─
Pea	--	--	--			─	─	─			--	--
Potato	••	••	••	••	••		─	─	─	••	••	••
Pumpkin	••	•							─	••	••	••
Radish	─	─	─	─	─	─	─	─	─	─	─	─
Rhubarb	--	─	─	─	─			--	--		--	--
Salsify	─	─	─							─	─	─
Scorzonera	─	─	─						─	─	─	─
Spinach	─	─	─	─	─	─	─	─	─	─	─	─
Swede	─	─	─						─	─	─	─
Sweet corn	--	--	--	--	--		─	─	─	--	--	--
Tomato							─	─	─	••	•	
Turnip	─	─	─							─	─	─

─── available fresh   ••• from store   - - - from freezer

150

Metric conversion tables

The following tables are a rough gardener's guide rather than a minutely accurate mathematical exercise.

Height & length

in	cm
¼	0.5
½	1
¾	2
1	2.5
1¼	3.5
1½	4
1¾	4.5
2	5
2¼	6
2½	6.5
2¾	7
3	8
3½	9
4	10
5	13
6	15
7	18
8	20
9	23
10	25
11	28
12 (1 ft)	30
14	35
15	38
16	40
18	45
20	50
24	60
28	70
30	75

ft	m
3	1
4	1.25
5	1.5
6	2
8	2.5
10	3
11	3.5
12	3.75
13	4
15	4.5
16	5
18	5.5
20	6
25	7.5
30	9
35	10.5
40	12
45	14
50	15

Weight

oz	g
¼	7
½	14
¾	21
1	30
1½	40
2	55
2½	70
3	85
3½	100
4	110
4½	130
5	140
6	170
7	200
8 (½ lb)	225
8¾	250 (¼ kg)
9	255
10	285
11	310
12	340
13	370
14	400
15	425
16 (1 lb)	450
17½	500 (½ kg)

lb	g/kg
1¼	560
1½	675
2	900
2¼	1 kg
3	1.6
4	1.8
4½	2
5	2.25
6	2.7
7	3.2
8	3.6
9	4.05
10	4.5

Capacity

pints	litres
¼	140 ml
½	285 ml
¾	425 ml
1	570 ml
1¼	710 ml
1½	850 ml
1¾	1 litre
2	1.2
3	1.75
4	2.5
5	3.0
6	3.4
7	4.0
1 gall	4.5 litres

Temperature

°F	°C
14	–10
23	–5
32	0
40	5
45	7
50	10
55	13
60	16
65	18
70	21
75	24
80	27
85	32

USEFUL ADDRESSES

SEEDSMEN
(Mail order – all issue free catalogues)

J.W. Boyce, 11 Soham, Ely, Cambridgeshire.

John Chambers, 15 Westleigh Road, Barton Seagrave, Kettering, Northants. (Herb seeds)

Samuel Dobie & Son Ltd., Upper Dee Mills, Llangollen, Clwyd.

Hurst Gunson Cooper Taber Ltd., Witham, Essex. (Garden seeds plus individual tailor-made cropping plan service)

S.E. Marshall & Co. Ltd., Regal Road, Wisbech, Cambridgeshire.

W. Robinson & Sons Ltd., Sunnybank, Forton, Preston, Lancashire. (Mammoth vegetable seeds for showing purposes)

Suttons Seeds Ltd., Hele Road, Torquay, Devon.

Thompson & Morgan Ltd., London Road, Ipswich, Suffolk.

Unwins Seeds Ltd., Seedsmen, Histon, Cambridge.

SPECIALIST NURSERYMEN
(Mail order)

C. Bowers, Westerby Farm, Outwell, Wisbech, Cambridgeshire. (Certified raspberry canes)

Highfield Nurseries, Whitminster, Gloucestershire. (Fruit trees and certified bushes, Cawood Delight rhubarb)

Kingsley Strawberries Ltd., Headley Mill Farm, Headley, Bordon, Hampshire. (Certified strawberries)

James McIntyre, Moyness Nurseries, Coupar Angus Road, Blairgowrie, Perthshire. (Certified fruit bushes and canes)

Donald McLean, Dornock Farm, Crieff, Perthshire. (Certified seed potatoes including many rare varieties)

Ken Muir, Honeypot Farm, Weeley Heath, Clacton-on-Sea, Essex. (Strawberries and cane fruits)

Thomas Rivers & Son, The Nurseries, Sawbridgeworth, Hertfordshire. (Fruit trees and certified bushes)

R.V. Roger, The Nurseries, Pickering, Yorkshire. (Fruit trees and certified bushes)

Scotts Nurseries, Merriott, Somerset. (Fruit trees and certified bushes including many rare varieties of top fruit)

W. Smith & Son Ltd., Hazlehead Garden Centre, Hazledene Road, Aberdeen. (Certified strawberries)

Springhill Nurseries Ltd., Lang Stracht, Aberdeen. (Certified fruit bushes and many rare varieties of gooseberry)

MISCELLANEOUS EQUIPMENT

ICI Garden Products – available in most garden centres (Corrugated or smooth plastic cloches)

Picken & Sons Ltd., Frankfort Street Works, Newtown, Birmingham. (Chase-type cloche wires)

Westray Cloches, 15 Church Road,

Upper Boddington, Daventry,
Northants. (Barn and tent types
fitted with netting)

Garden frames
Access Frames, Yelverton Road,
Crick, Northampton.

Halls Homes & Gardens Ltd.,
Church Road, Paddock Wood,
Kent.

Fruit cages
Agriframes Ltd., Charlwoods
Road, East Grinstead, Sussex.

Knowle Nets, East Road, Bridport,
Dorset.

Fertilisers
Chempak Ltd., Brewhouse Lane,
Hertford.

Maskells Fertilisers, Dirleton
Works, Stephenson Street,
London E16.

Phostrogen Ltd., Corwen, Clwyd.

SPECIALIST SOCIETIES

Herb Society, 34 Boscobel Place,
London SW1.

Henry Doubleday Research
Association, Convent Lane,
Bocking, Braintree, Essex.
(Organic gardening association)

National Society of Leisure
Gardeners Ltd., 22 High Street,
Flitwick, Bedfordshire. (The
'allotment holders' society; will
offer much information and
advice.)

National Vegetable Society,
W.R. Hargreaves, 29 Revidge
Road, Blackburn, Lancashire.

Northern Horticultural Society,
Harlow Car Gardens, Harrogate,
North Yorkshire.

Royal Horticultural Society,
Vincent Square, London SW1.

The Soil Association, Walnut Tree
Manor, Haughley, Stowmarket,
Suffolk. (Organic gardening
association)

FURTHER READING

Baker, Harry. *Royal Horticultural Society's Encyclopaedia of Practical Gardening: Fruit.* Mitchell Beazley, 1980.

Biggs, Tony. *Royal Horticultural Society's Encyclopaedia of Practical Gardening: Vegetables.* Mitchell Beazley, 1980.

British Agrochemicals Association. *Directory of Garden Chemicals.* Alembic House, 93 Albert Embankment, London SE1 7TU. Published annually.

Brooks, Audrey and Halstead, Andrew. *Royal Horticultural Society's Encyclopaedia of Practical Gardening: Garden Pests and Diseases.* Mitchell Beazley, 1980.

Dampney, Janet and Pomeroy, Elizabeth. *All About Herbs.* Hamlyn, 1977.

Ellis, Audrey. *All About Home Freezing.* Hamlyn, 1975.

Hills, Lawrence D. *Organic Gardening.* Penguin, 1977.

Larkcom, Joy. *Vegetables from Small Gardens.* Faber, 1976. *Salads the Year Round.* Hamlyn, 1980.

Royal Horticultural Society. *The Fruit Garden Displayed.* 1975. *The Vegetable Garden Displayed.* 1982.

Salter, P.J. and Bleasdale, J.K.A. *Know and Grow Vegetables.* Oxford University Press, 1979.

Simons, Arthur J. *The New Vegetable Grower's Handbook.* Penguin, 1975.

Titchmarsh, Alan. *Gardening Under Cover.* Hamlyn, 1979. *Pest-Free Plants.* Marks & Spencer, 1982. *Royal Horticultural Society's Encyclopaedia of Practical Gardening: Gardening Techniques.* Mitchell Beazley, 1981.

Walls, Ian G. *A-Z of Garden Pests and Problems.* Collins, 1979.

Whitehead, George. *Growing for Showing.* Faber, 1978.

INDEX

NOTES

It is difficult to remember from one
season to the next how well your
chosen varieties have performed. Use
these pages to note sowing times and
weather conditions which could have
been responsible for the success or
failure of the crop.